Humane Leadership

Humane Leadership

Lead With Radical Love, Be a Kick-Ass Boss

Marcel Schwantes

BEP

BUSINESS EXPERT PRESS

Leader in applied, concise business books

Humane Leadership: Lead With Radical Love, Be a Kick-Ass Boss

First published in 2025 by
Business Expert Press, LLC
222 East 46th Street, New York, NY 10017
www.businessexpertpress.com

ISBN-13: 978-1-63742-782-8 (paperback)
ISBN-13: 978-1-63742-783-5 (e-book)

Business Expert Press Human Resource Management and Organizational Behavior Collection

First edition: 2025

10 9 8 7 6 5 4 3 2 1

EU SAFETY REPRESENTATIVE
Mare Nostrum Group B.V.
Mauritskade 21D
1091 GC Amsterdam
The Netherlands
gpsr@mare-nostrum.co.uk

For my son Joseph: may you become the leader the world you're growing up in desperately needs. May you embrace the principles of Love in Action.

For the woman I married and adore: You are the embodiment of radical Love in Action. I dedicate this book to you.

Description

What if the secret to being an outstanding leader lies in radical love?

One morning, Marcel Schwantes stepped out of the shower and collapsed in agony, paralyzed from the waist down. When he called his boss to explain his situation, he was accused of insubordination.

This moment marked the culmination of a two-year struggle in what should have been a season of learning and growth in an executive-level HR role with a promising future. Instead, he faced immense stress, disengagement, and a toxic work environment that nearly destroyed his career.

In *Humane Leadership: Lead with Radical Love, Be a Kick-Ass Boss*, the author offers a revolutionary perspective, advocating for a radical shift toward love and humanity. Drawing on personal experiences, case studies, and compelling research, he reveals how leaders can transform organizations by embracing genuine care for their employees.

Schwantes explains the five principles of effective leadership: patience, kindness, humility, advocacy, and trustworthiness. It offers a practical guide to leading teams with actionable love and care so people, businesses, and organizations flourish.

This book is for anyone seeking to create a thriving, motivated team and become a truly kick-ass boss in today's chaotic world.

Contents

Testimonials

"For years I've been saying that leadership is love. In this must-read book, Marcel Schwantes explains why leaders must adopt love as a business strategy. Backed by data and case studies, this step-by-step guide will show you how to put love to work—and reap wonderful personal, professional, and financial rewards as a result."—**Ken Blanchard, coauthor of *The New One Minute Manager* and *The Simple Truths of Leadership***

*"*Humane Leadership *is an essential guide for anyone looking to navigate the complexities of modern leadership with compassion and integrity. Schwantes›s personal narrative and deeply insightful analysis provide a compelling case for why humane leadership is not just an option, but a necessity in today's world. Through his own experiences and the struggles he faced, Schwantes illustrates the profound impact that empathetic and servant leadership can have on organizational culture and employee engagement. This book is a beacon for leaders at all levels, offering practical strategies and inspiring a shift toward a more compassionate and effective leadership style. Highly recommended for those who aspire to lead with heart and achieve sustainable success."*—**Dr. Marshall Goldsmith, Thinkers 50 #1 Executive Coach and *New York Times* bestselling author of *The Earned Life, Triggers, and What Got You Here Won't Get You There***

"After reading Marcel Schwantes's inspiring new book, Humane Leadership, *I was reminded of one of my favorite quotes from J.R.R. Tolkien: 'I have found that it is the small everyday deeds of ordinary folks that keep the darkness at bay. Small acts of kindness and love.' Marcel beautifully embraces this idea throughout his book as he provides a proven framework showing that all of us perform significantly better—and have greater well-being—when we are treated with respect and "actionable love." This pivotal book is vitally needed today as so many are more doubtful and starved for belonging than ever before. A life-altering read!"*—**Stephen M. R. Covey, *The New York Times* and #1 *Wall Street Journal* bestselling author of *The Speed of Trust* and *Trust & Inspire***

"Humane Leadership *gets to the heart of what's missing in today's workplaces: people don't feel valued, cared for and part of the shared purpose. Schwantes' insightful book illustrates what's possible when leaders create workplaces centered on care, collaboration and human connection: your team members and your business* thrive!—**Bob Chapman, CEO of Barry–Wehmiller and author of *Everybody Matters: The Extraordinary Power of Caring for Your People Like Family***

"*Marcel Schwantes masterfully blends personal insights, rigorous research and thoughtful analysis to create a compelling blueprint for effective leadership. This book not only challenges conventional wisdom but provides a roadmap for developing workplaces where compassion and efficiency coexist harmoniously.*"—**Hubert Joly, former Best Buy CEO, senior lecturer, Harvard Business School, Author, *The Heart of Business***

"*In a world craving authentic connection, Marcel Schwantes's approach is timely and necessary. This book is a must-read for leaders who want to lead with empathy and compassion.*"—**Frances Frei, Professor, Harvard Business School**

"*Marcel Schwantes brings an indispensable touch of humanity to our understanding of leadership. Anyone interested in improving their own or other people's leadership talent should read this book carefully and follow his sage advice.*" —**Tomas Chamorro-Premuzic, author, *Why Do So Many Incompetent Men Become Leaders?: (And How to Fix It)***

"*Leading with love and care isn't just an idea; it's a movement, and Marcel Schwantes is at its forefront. His book provides practical wisdom for leaders who aim to foster well-being, belonging, inclusion, and engagement.*"—**Howard Behar, Retired president of Starbucks Coffee Company and author of *It's Not About the Coffee***

"Humane Leadership *is well-researched, insightful, and pragmatic. Spoiler Alert: Love wins!* —**Mark Miller, *Wall Street Journal* and International Best-selling Author of *Culture Rules* and former VP of High Performance Leadership at Chick-fil-A, Inc.**

"People create value in organizations making colleague development essential. In this innovative and entirely practical book, Marcel Schwantes argues that those who lead with love have highly motivated teams and better financial performance, and he shows readers precisely what to do to lead with love."— **Paul J. Zak, PhD, author of *Immersion: The Science of the Extraordinary and the Source of Happiness***

"Marcel Schwantes masterfully illustrates that true leadership comes from the heart. His book serves as both an inspirational and practical resource, guiding leaders to lead with kindness, empathy, and love."—**Robb Holman, Inside Out Leadership Catalyst, Global Speaker, and 4x Author**

"Leading with practical love and care is not just a philosophy—it's a strategy for success. Marcel Schwantes's book is a beacon for leaders who want to make a lasting impact."—**Robert Glazer, #1 WSJ and USA Today Bestseller of *Elevate* and *Elevate Your Team*.**

*"*Humane Leadership *reveals how compassionate leadership cultivates a flourishing, committed workforce. Blending practical strategies with compelling narratives, it taps into timeless wisdom to demonstrate the transformative power of empathy in management. Essential reading for leaders seeking to build a culture where kindness and excellence coexist."*—**Raj Sisodia, Cofounder, Conscious Capitalism Inc., FEMSA Distinguished University Professor of Conscious Enterprise, Tecnologico de Monterrey**

"This book builds an evidence-based case that love, the action verb, can catapult leaders to unprecedented success. Marcel Schwantes provides five pivotal practices that we can put to work now for better results. The marketplace is yearning for a generation of humane leaders who foster a place of both care and high performance. Will you be one of them?"—**Cheryl Bachelder, Former CEO, Popeyes Louisiana Kitchen, Inc., Author, *Dare to Serve***

"Marcel Schwantes thoughtfully captures the essence of human (and humane) leadership. This book serves as a heartfelt manual for creating kindness-centered workplaces where people truly matter."—**Houston Kraft, cofounder of CharacterStrong and author of *Deep Kindness***

"Marcel Schwantes's Humane Leadership *is a groundbreaking exploration of how leaders must evolve to meet the needs of an increasingly complex and disconnected workplace. By putting love into practice, leaders can shift from simply being human to being truly humane—and, in the process, combat disengagement, dissatisfaction, and unwanted attrition. This is an indispensable playbook for anyone looking to harness love as a strategic leadership tool."*—**Julie Winkle Giulioni, author of *Promotions Are SO Yesterday* and coauthor of *Help Them Grow or Watch Them Go***

"Marcel Schwantes brilliantly provides principles and strategies grounded in agape love to build businesses that put our humanity and the Earth at their center, not simply profit. And what could be more needed?"—**Jacqueline Novogratz, Founder and CEO, Acumen**

Foreword

My Story—A Kid's Dream About Work

It was spring of 1982 and I was second guessing some big choices I had made in life. I was 24 years old and about to graduate with honors from the University of Michigan with a master's degree in Computer Engineering. I began to doubt that this career would be satisfying and productive. Maybe I chose the wrong course of study. I had done enough professional work in the software industry by this point that I knew there was trouble. I wasn't sure I was ready for a career of it.

As I walked the streets of downtown Ann Arbor, Michigan, I paused and pictured what I wanted. In my mind's eye, I saw a big open room, a brick loft, with lots of sunshine, a team of people deeply engaged in the pursuit of important work. They were having fun, they were collaborating, there was palpable human energy in the room.

That was all I needed to get back to work, complete my degree, and start my professional life. That momentary imagery gave me hope because I could see the future that I wanted to create and be a part of. If I could imagine it, it was possible.

I put that idea in a small box on a shelf in the back of mind and got on with life.

The Pursuit of Joy

You are here for a reason.

You picked up a book on humane leadership because you are yearning for change in your work life. Something is bothering you. You can't quite put your finger on it, but it is there, and you are searching for an answer, something different. You're not exactly sure what it is or how you'll find it.

Your search has led you here, to this book and these pages. I urge you not to turn away. You've come to the right place. Keep reading.

You see, I was once exactly where you are now. By my mid-30s I wanted to get as far away from my work life as I could, but that was not a practical idea. Work was how I kept a roof over our heads, and how we would save for college for our young daughters. Work had become a means to an end. I wanted more from my work life than what I was getting. I knew I couldn't keep going the way I was going for another 30 years. Something had to give and I didn't want it to be me.

So, I began my search. I started reading. I read about excellence. I read about management. I read about systems thinking. I read about success. Those books were encouraging. They pointed to examples of organizations that achieved much better and sustainable results. That was helpful, but I still wanted more. I wanted to be thrilled about my work and the team of people around me. I wanted human energy. I wanted camaraderie. I wanted teamwork. And yes, results, success, more sanity and less chaos too. However, I believed those things would be an outcome of a compelling and energizing work culture, not the goal.

I wanted joy and love in my work. I wasn't going to stop until I got it.

Our Purpose Is Our Joy

I believe humans are wired for three things:

1. We are built to work. Hard work done well is fulfilling.
2. We are wired to work together. At our core, we are relational beings.
3. We are wired to achieve big things. We all want to work on something bigger than ourselves.

On top of all this, we operate at our best when we are serving others. Our purpose is to serve others with the work of our hearts, our hands, our minds. This is why we join companies or form them. It's why we build teams and processes for those teams to work well together. It's why we appreciate quality.

Above all, when we are recognized for what we do for others through gratitude and delight, we experience a profound joy.

Who Can Lead?

Perhaps you are already a leader. Most of us are, even if we don't have the title or the box on the org chart that says so. All of us can lead from anywhere. We don't need a title, a corner office, or a "box" with our name in it.

Leadership is about influencing others.
Leadership is about creating the conditions for success.
Leadership is about ... leading!

The Negative Lessons

How do we learn to lead? Perhaps some of us are born leaders, but most of us have to try things and see if they work. This can be a painfully slow process and if it ends up being too slow or too painful, we lose patience and stamina and we stop.

I learned to lead in a work environment from one of my early bosses. His goal seemed to be to get me to work lots of overtime and he was not concerned about me spending time with my family. He discouraged taking vacations. If I spoke about the desire to produce high-quality software, he'd tell me, "Don't worry about that, we'll have plenty of time to fix things later." We never did.

This cycle of ship it then fix it led to tons of firefighting and low morale.

Fear was rampant.

This is how I learned to lead. By necessity, I became a hero, a firefighter, and I spent a lot of time in meetings prioritizing problems. We had to prioritize them because we could never fix all of them.

As I climbed the corporate ladder, I became the example for others to follow as I was now promoting them into leadership positions. I led with fear, and I taught them to do the same. What other way was there? I had never seen one.

Fear Is Not the Leadership Answer

I will say it clearly: *Fear does not work.* Especially if it is *artificial* fear created with false flags, irrational goals, and impossible deadlines. Fear kills any chance we have for succeeding. Fear-based management may be one of the most common approaches in business today. Given its prevalence, I often wonder if there are classes in business school that teach it. I suppose a possible answer is that our education system itself is a fear-based system.

Take, for example, the crazy system of force ranking a workforce and then cutting the lowest 10 percent on the rating scale year after year. Imagine what happens in this world. Your workforce spends most of their time trying to get a good ranking and making sure at least 10 percent of their peers won't. The outcome is so obviously predictable, it is amazing to me how long such systems continue to persist.

The Leader's Job

A leader's job is to pump fear *out* of the room, not in.

One of the books my dad made sure he put in our hands was *Aesop's Fables.* I loved reading them and read them again and again. Sour Grapes, the Tortoise and The Hare, The Boy Who Cried Wolf, The Town Mouse and the Country Mouse ... every one of these incredibly short, meaningful tales contained an important life lesson about effort, humility, patience, openness, diversity ... in short, my dad thought this would be one great way to teach his kids values and ethics. He was right.

The story that really stuck with me, though, was likely a lesser known one from the more famous mentioned previously:

The Wind and The Sun

The Wind and the Sun were disputing which was the stronger.

Suddenly they saw a traveler coming down the road, and the Sun said:

"I see a way to decide our dispute. Whichever of us can cause that traveler to take off his cloak shall be regarded as the stronger. You begin."

So, the Sun retired behind a cloud, and the Wind began to blow as hard as it could upon the traveler.

But the harder he blew the more closely did the traveler wrap his cloak round him, till at last the Wind gave up in despair.

Then the Sun came out and shone in all his glory upon the traveler, who soon found it too hot to walk with his cloak on.

If there was a core value upon which I would ultimately build my leadership life, and in doing so inspire those I led, it was this: love wins every time; particularly if the victory you seek is different than busy-ness, and yes-ness, and obedience. If you want engagement ... if you want your team to lead even when you are not there, then only *love in action* will work. Not fear, not intimidation, not bullying, or bravado, and not by being the "smartest guy in the room."

What Is Needed Now

In this age of artificial intelligence, machine learning, big data, and robotics, we humans are beginning to question where we fit in this new technologically sophisticated landscape and is there still a place for most of us in the work world.

I can assure you there is!

However, what we need most right now is what is still only (and forever will be) in the human domain: creativity, imagination, invention, and innovation. These are the things that separate us from our machines. There is no company or team on the planet that says: *we need less of those four things.*

And the most important point is this: Those four elements of our humanity come from a place in our brain that literally shuts down when we are afraid. Fear robs us of our most important differentiator. It takes away our humanity and keeps us in reptile brain.

The companies, the team, the leaders that learn to be humane in their leadership will pull away from those that don't. Those organizations will double down on fear and ultimately disappear. Many of the leaders in those organizations will blame their demise on something else, some external force, and will have avoided learning the most important leadership lesson of all: we did it to ourselves.

You will not be one of those leaders because you are seeking out books like this. Congratulations. You have taken the first big step on an important and meaningful journey to joy.

Many people will thank you for your courage.

Dream Fulfilled

Sometime in 2007, I was returning to our office in downtown Ann Arbor after a meeting. It was mid-morning and the place was alive with the hum and buzz of the human energy of our team. Sunlight was streaming through the skylights of our brick loft, and it hit me.

You did it! This is it! You achieved the dream of the 24 year old. The little box on the back shelf of my mind reopened like a gift 25 years later. I had never thought about that dream until that moment and it gave me chills to see how perfectly I had imagined the company I had helped create.

Your dreams can come true.

The Door Is Now Open ... Walk Through It

The *future of work is human AND humane*. The future of work IS about love in action. Marcel Schwantes wrote a book to inspire you on a joyful journey of your own. Help make the world a better place by becoming the leader you always knew you could be.

This book will help you get started.

Richard B. Sheridan
CEO, cofounder, Chief Storyteller
Menlo Innovations
Ann Arbor, Michigan
Author of *Joy, Inc—How We Built a Workplace People Love* and *Chief Joy Officer—How Great Leaders Elevate Human Energy and Eliminate Fear*

Acknowledgments

Writing this book has been a five-year journey that I could not have completed without the support and assistance of many individuals.

First and foremost, my deepest gratitude to my wife, Noelle. I could not have done this without you. Your role in this journey was not just about cheering me on but about being my rock. Your unwavering support, prayers, and encouragement, through the highs and lows, were instrumental in this journey. Your belief in me was the fuel that kept me going. I love you.

I am deeply grateful to many of my mentors, coaches, and teachers through the years, whose leadership, wisdom, insights, and "forward nudges" were invaluable throughout my growth as a leader, entrepreneur, and a human being: Bruce Nelson, Elizabeth Talbot, Paul Crampton, Terry Massey, Alex Lavidge, Mike Bradshaw, Mike Vacanti, Kevin Monroe, Marty Miller, David Achata, Robb Holman, and Andy Nash.

Thanks to the Wednesday Morning Men's Group for your support, friendship, prayers, and caffeinated laughter.

Kudos to the many experts and sages—many of whom have come to share their world-changing ideas on my podcast and who have chosen to endorse this book—for your wisdom over the years.

Getting a book published is a daunting multilayered process. Special thanks to my literary agent, Kelli Christiansen, for believing in my message and expertly walking me through an exhausting book proposal development. A heartfelt load of gratitude and praise to my developmental editor and book coach, Ariel Curry. Your seamless approach to bringing clarity and purpose to each chapter in our brainstorming sessions and your feedback have not just improved but transformed this book.

To Richard Sheridan, who graciously accepted my invitation to write the foreword. Your book, *Chief Joy Officer*, has been a catalyst in expanding the Corinthians account into a comprehensive leadership framework for real-life business application. I am grateful for your leadership expertise and the ideas presented in this book.

A big thank you to my publisher, Business Expert Press, who saw in my manuscript what other publishers didn't and for sharing this labor of love with the world.

My heartfelt and endless gratitude to Barry Johnson. Your exceptional talent, vision, patience, and dedication in designing the artwork and book cover through its many iterations is awe-inspiring. Your creativity (did I mention patience?) and ability to envision things in ways I couldn't have made this a visually engaging book. I see you, Barry!

Sincere gratitude to Kay Johnson for her expertise in developing curriculum and crafting training and workshop elements that accompany this book. What a gem of a find you've been!

A thousand thank yous to Zac and Megan Ingraham for igniting the flame and partnering with me to create what will surely become one of the best Substack platforms on the Web! (See the QR code under my biography on page 203 and subscribe for free tools and resources.)

To my friends, family, and colleagues who provided feedback, shared ideas, and cheered me on—your support has meant the world to me. Thank you all.

Finally, I'm forever grateful for The Way, who makes all things work together for good.

Introduction

One morning, as I stepped out of the shower to get ready for work, my lower back locked up completely, and I crashed to the floor, paralyzed from the waist down. I crawled on my elbows in agonizing pain to grab the phone in another room. My first call was to the CEO, one of a handful of bosses to whom I reported. In a state of panic, I told her that I was severely injured and would have to pull myself out of a major project I was supposed to be leading, one under her guidance as my preceptor. I lay on my stomach in the living room, inches from a carpet that obviously needed vacuuming. Stars circled my head as I struggled to curb the pain, and I heard accusations of insubordination on the other end. I knew this was the last straw—no matter how good my reason. I was on the chopping block.

If you feel like you've stepped into a movie with a plot getting thicker by the minute, don't worry; there's quite a background to this storyline. Depending on one's perspective, some might even cast me as the villain. After all, I was seen in the eyes of my superiors as a rogue employee with a personal agenda.

The year was 2002, and I was accepted into a prestigious human resources (HR) administrative residency program working for a hospital in the United States. The two-year program had me rotate through the different HR functions to learn the "best practices" and eventually get hired in a human resources management position at one of the parent company's hospitals. For each of those rotations, a preceptor—a department head of each respective HR function and the CEO—was assigned to mentor me in their areas of expertise. My position of "HR Resident" reported to an interim HR director—a dominant external consultant (referred to as "The Consultant" from here on). The hospital contracted her to keep the HR department from imploding while hospital administration searched for a new, full-time HR director.

Donning her traditional blue blazer and standing six feet tall in high heels, The Consultant's commanding presence exuded confidence and urgency wherever she walked. I recall the quiet productivity of my busy co-workers, often startled by The Consultant's bold entrance into the room, the wind of her momentum trailing behind her as her thick heels pounded against the floor.

After a successful first rotation, I began to take mental notes of my surroundings as the honeymoon phase of my residency wore off. I noticed department managers—my future preceptors—appeared unhappy, stressed, and frustrated; they worked long hours, hardly spoke up, and spent most of their work hours putting out fires and attending meetings. The meetings became a dumping ground for complaints at the expense of the underperforming HR department. Managers would leave these meetings discouraged and overwhelmed. It soon became apparent that my preceptors weren't available for my mentoring sessions, which was the whole intent of the residency program. They often looked bewildered, disengaged, and too scared to provide value. I quickly understood that they were reluctant—even resentful—to have been placed into a preceptor role for my development when they lacked resources, support, and training for their own professional development. Most of them dealt with their displeasure and managed their workload by handing me menial, low-level tasks to keep me doing "busy work" so they could get real work done.

By the third rotation into the employee benefits area of HR, I felt mentally and emotionally disengaged from the residency myself. On paper, it looked promising; in the trenches, it lacked meaning and purpose, leadership, and direction. I started to drift off from a lack of motivation and merely put in the minimum effort required to complete my daily tasks and collect a paycheck. I dragged myself to work, wondering the point of it all.

As you dive into my story, you might recognize some patterns. They're not uncommon. They're the kind that millions of hardworking folks face, leading to stress, anxiety, and yes, sometimes even trauma. I know because I've been through it.

The Disengaged Worker

The Gallup Organization, which has polled the world's employees and managers, revealed in their State of the Global Workplace 2023 Report that only 31 percent of employees in the United States and Canada were "thriving at work," meaning they were engaged. These are your high performers who are involved in, enthusiastic about, and committed to their work. Fifty-two percent of them were "quiet quitting," or disengaged. These are your employees who show up and kill time, do the minimum required with rare extra effort. These are the people thinking about lunch and waiting for the clock to hit 5 p.m. You don't want to hear what the remaining workers do. OK, I'll tell you, but don't shoot the messenger. Gallup reports that 17 percent were "loud quitting," another term for "actively disengaged." These employees aren't just unhappy at work; they're busy acting out their unhappiness. Every day, these workers undermine what their engaged co-workers accomplish. And they may be working for you right now, infecting your staff's morale.

I was clearly in the 52 percent group, merely going through the motions, sleepwalking through my workday, putting time—but not energy or passion—into my work. This wasn't something I had experienced up to that point in my young corporate career. I've always been a type-A self-starter and proactive when faced with a challenge. If you've ever taken the DiSC personality assessment, my behavioral styles are "dominance" and "influence." The former is known for boldness and self-assurance—pursuing tough challenges with assertiveness. This style can also easily irritate others with their opposing points of view. The latter style is a people-oriented style of both bold and accepting. They are motivated by their connections with others, pursue warm relationships, and invite collaboration and community.

In the absence of guidance and support, I decided to take matters into my own hands and make changes to the residency program that would benefit my professional development while also serving the hospital's mission. Although this was partly due to my personality, my intentions were positive, and I wanted to improve the situation. I added a hospital rotation focused on leadership development into the program that was not originally "on paper."

I took my strategy to The Consultant to get her buy-in and state my case so that my intentions didn't come across as full belligerence in her eyes. Over a tense meal that caused acrobats in my stomach, I explained to her that I wasn't being developed to the standards required for a leadership role within HR. The program she designed was failing because the people entrusted to mentor me had no capacity or time to lead and guide me under such unfavorable circumstances.

"They are also failing under enormous pressure to make their own deadlines and meet performance expectations. They are overworked and overstretched," I told her, surprised by the boldness of my delivery. I explained that leadership development, one of the most critical functions under the HR umbrella, was absent from the program. I saw my proposed rotation as an opportunity to do something special by partnering with the newly promoted Director of Leadership Development, someone I was closely familiar with and admired.

"That's not an area that falls under the HR structure of the program that I designed," said The Consultant sternly. "You can't just change the program by cherry-picking what you feel will benefit your development."

"I'm asking that we *include* it as a part of the HR function," I said. "This is an area I'm particularly interested in and one that will benefit hospital managers. I know I can make an immediate impact by helping develop training and pull together resources to make better leaders here," I concluded. "There's immense value in this. They need it, and I need it."

Looking back, I realized that The Consultant was more focused on protecting her own interests and territory than considering the bigger picture of what I proposed. She created the program structure, got buy-in from the CEO, and was determined to plow ahead. Any attempt to change direction now would undermine her authority. Despite my desire to negotiate a new strategy and make progress, she insisted on complete compliance with her own ideas and methods. I ultimately realized that I had to act without her support to pursue what I felt without a shadow of a doubt was the right thing to do—take control of my own career path. Just one year in, I was headed for a showdown that positioned my integrity and dignity against the iron fist of an autocratic boss.

The second year of the residency began with the newly inserted leadership development rotation—without The Consultant's approval. The Director of Leadership Development welcomed my role and groomed me to serve in one of the hospital's most needed functions. It was a great fit that played to my strengths and talents, and I began to thrive for the first time. I finally felt empowered, energized, and engaged in my work. I was making a difference and received compliments from hospital managers for my work everywhere I walked inside the hospital grounds.

The fact that my program was working only exacerbated the strain on my relationship with The Consultant.

Breaking away from The Consultant's version of the residency was a clear act of corporate rebellion in her eyes; I wasn't subservient and didn't fall in line. Soon after, she started to campaign for my termination. The Consultant succeeded in her smear campaign. Her inner circle—the people with the most power, right up to the hospital CEO—believed her side of the story without bringing me into the discussion to listen and seek my perspective, identify the roadblocks, clear the path, and perhaps negotiate a viable solution to everyone's liking. I was denigrated and became the central villain in the now-official narrative put out by those in power.

The Breaking Point

The Consultant pulled her inner circle into toxic groupthink. If you're not familiar with it, groupthink is a psychological phenomenon in which individual members of small groups often conform to a perceived consensus, regardless of their personal beliefs about its validity, correctness, or truth. It can be dangerous because it often leads to errors in decision-making. The group usually takes on the ideas of one person of influence and/or a small group of people who hold power over the rest of the group. Team members don't speak up in autocratic environments, mainly out of fear.

As groupthink intensified, so did the tension in the atmosphere. The Consultant had one last trick up her sleeve to display her power. She convinced the hospital's CEO to drop me into a lead role in a high-level, complex, and multilayered project with several milestones. It would require facilitating ongoing strategy meetings with a council of hospital leaders and board approval before implementation. I knew I was way over my head without prior experience to lead such a large project without a strong preceptor—and The Consultant knew it, too.

Initially, I had hope. This project, after all, meant exposure at the executive level that would stretch my development in a new area. My hopes soon began to wane. The Consultant assigned the CEO as my preceptor for the project and instructed her and key project members to cut off communication when I sought assistance or asked for direction. I received radio silence to meeting requests, and when I spontaneously showed up at someone's desk to ask a question and seek advice, I would get poker faces and be told they couldn't help me. The more desperate I became, the less support I received. I felt like I was starring in an episode of the Twilight Zone.

Since I had communicated a prior desire for more autonomy and ownership, The Consultant gave me some freedom, but with a twisted objective: strip me of preceptors, support, and mentoring and see if I would sink or swim.

I sank—not figuratively, but literally.

As the pressure mounted to conform to their standards and perform to their expectations to lead the project team, immense stress wreaked havoc on my body. I face-planted on the bathroom floor of my apartment as I stepped out of the shower, unable to move.

After checking myself into the emergency department of a local hospital (not the one I worked for), the ER physician asked me to rate my stress at work on a scale of 1 to 10. I told him, "25." He nodded and wasn't a bit surprised. He called my condition stress and anxiety related. He explained that people may experience psychological distress as physical pain, a process known as somatization. The pain is real but does not result from any physical condition or injury.

I spent a month laying horizontally, unable to move from the waist down, and soon filed for work disability. After rehabilitating my body and emotional state for another month, I returned to the hospital to finish my two-year residency. As soon as I returned, The Consultant, the CEO, and the interim HR director began a witch-hunt to get me fired unless I wrote a letter of apology to the hospital's CEO for my act of "insubordination" (removing myself from the project lead role). I complied and submitted to whatever they demanded to keep my peace of mind and a low profile. There were other attempts to terminate me if I didn't submit my will to their authority.

On a positive note, even though there were moments I wanted to resign, once the smoke cleared the air, I successfully finished the two-year residency program and moved on, but The Consultant left an indelible mark; it took months to recover from the trauma.

Various experiences can cause work trauma and are more common than we realize. It can lead to a state of chronic stress response. In other words, people who have been traumatized can become stuck in a constant state of stress and anxiety. This is like revving up a car engine while the car is in park, straining the engine until it eventually breaks down. Similarly, when the human body is constantly revved up to a state of high stress, it can lead to burnout and impair well-being and performance.

After this traumatic episode, I became interested in understanding what causes someone competent in her field and respected by other executives to act inhumanely with people who have less power or positional authority. Thus began my journey into understanding what makes a true leader worth following.

A few months after I left the hospital and had time to heal physically and emotionally and reflect on the residency, another hospital nearby hired me for a director position. It was a fresh start, and I reported to an executive with a distinctively different management style. He became, for me, the ideal model of leadership, and his leadership actions, practices, and behaviors, which I outline in Chapter 1, have been confirmed by scientific and anecdotal evidence that I will illustrate throughout this book.

The Power of Love in Action

When we loosely throw the word love around in casual conversation, it's perfectly natural to express it regarding certain people, places, and things. Think about it. It's acceptable to profess love for a favorite sports team—for whom you might spend a few hours a week rooting. I have no problems sharing with others that I love my Los Angeles Dodgers and "bleed Dodger blue." Professing love for the college or university we attended is acceptable. It's even perfectly acceptable to exclaim our love for a special pair of jeans we might wear only a few times a year. In the workplace, we may go home and proudly tell our loved ones, "I love my job," or "I love my co-workers." But leaders aren't always comfortable expressing love for a team of people they oversee. They may spend nearly half their waking hours with their employees doing good work to the satisfaction of customers, yet they find it hard to infuse the word "love" into the business lexicon. To me, that type of thinking is bizarre. For every leader ashamed of or fearful of mixing love with work, I point to 10 others whose leadership behaviors unabashedly demonstrate love for their team, company, customers, culture, and everything they contribute to the world.

While I'm certainly an idealist, this book is far from depicting the workplace in some Utopian, Norman Rockwell portrait of the perfect corporate life. You must do your part by stretching your thinking to reimagine the possibilities for a more loving, human-centered, and humane workplace that results in profitable outcomes. For example, what if you saw your colleague, co-worker, or direct report as real people with real hopes, dreams, and fears as crucial as your own? And what if, one day, you decided to connect to the heart of people at work as you would a good friend, as one human being caring for another?

As you imagine being in this frame of mind, let me ask you this: How would the dynamics change in the workplace as you encountered new challenges and solved complex business problems with the very folks you are kind to and care about? I believe the workplace and how we conduct "business as usual" would radically differ.

This is especially true if you're in a leadership role, whether you're the shift lead supervisor of five people on the manufacturing floor, the founder of a 50-person start-up, or a Fortune 500 company CEO. Leaders have an enormous responsibility to care for people entrusted to their care. Bob Chapman, coauthor of *Everybody Matters* and CEO of Barry–Wehmiller, a $3.6 billion global company, reminded me in a conversation I had with him that every employee is somebody's daughter or son or someone's spouse or partner. And each person relies on the leader for guidance—to be cared for, protected, and feel like they belong to a community. Sounds familiar? Think back to your upbringing. Babies and children require love, care, and protection in a nurturing environment for them to thrive. That's where it all starts. Love begins as a human development process in the brain as infants are exposed to positive bonding experiences in loving homes. As we mature, hopefully, into healthy and productive adults ready to take on the world, we remain social animals, requiring the need to receive social and emotional stability through relationships and community.[1]

People also want to experience purpose, growth, and success in their jobs and feel that their leaders are doing their best to care for them. That's the bottom line: People want to feel cared for. But I call it for what it really is: *People want to feel loved.*

This book offers leaders a practical guide to leading their teams or workforce with actionable love and care so that their people, business, and organization will flourish. As you turn the pages, consider the ensuing provocation of your thoughts like peeling layers of an onion. You're going to need some coaxing and convincing first to believe that love, in the right business context, does indeed matter for leadership. Chapters 1 and 2 will serve in the capacity of challenging your belief system. The chapters beyond that will present a practical framework for leading through Love in Action.

Why Should You Care?

Why write a business book about leading with love in such a loveless business world where people are objectified as a means to a profitable end and takers far outnumber givers? Why should we even care? It's business, and this is how we conduct ourselves at work, nothing personal; get over it, right? I beg to differ. Perhaps we should ask this: Why do people lead in ways so unsuitable to how humans are innately designed to want to experience positive emotions? In Chapter 1, I sound the alarm and cite research explaining that toxic work environments still prevalent today are killing us, literally.

A Surprising Turn

As I examined the literature and case studies on human development and performance, I explored another unfamiliar route for a business leadership book. What if, I asked myself, what the world's noble religions have known for thousands of years about the practice of "love for one another" (even if you don't practice religion or consider yourself agnostic or atheist) may be the key to unlocking the potential of the world's business leaders to perform at an unprecedented human level? This is where my research took an interesting and surprising turn. Love is a human requirement for our very survival. Our need for it transcends countries, cultures, generations, and humanity. The world's religions understand the importance of love. For example, "agape love" is charitable, selfless, altruistic, and unconditional in Christian circles. It's the kind of love described by St. Thomas Aquinas as having a desire for another to succeed, or "to will the good of another." In Jewish tradition, the commandment to love other people is given in the Torah, which states, "Love your neighbor like yourself." The Qur'an urges Muslims to treat all people with "deep kindness." The Bahá'í Faith describes four types of love, including the love of human beings for human beings. And in Buddhist and Hindu traditions, "karuṇā" love is practiced through compassion and mercy—a selfless form of love to reduce the suffering of others.

We take for granted what we have historically known and experienced as outdated conventional management standards of practice from the Industrial Age. But, as preposterous as it may sound, what if we turned to the virtues of altruistic love, as taught by the world's religions, to inform and transform leaders in the workplace?

When I inspected the contrarian possibilities of turning to religion instead of science for answers to workplace problems, I was dumbfounded by the discoveries that connect both: Religion in its purest form, outside the context of dogma and fundamentalism that divide the masses, has defined the most altruistic human traits for people belonging in faith communities, in relationship to each other. On the other hand, science has demonstrated the evidence for raising the bar on leadership, organizational, and human performance to energize teams and maximize profit.

As it turns out, the discoveries of both are aligned. What religions have known about virtuous human traits, science has studied and confirmed its impact on people and work cultures. As distant as they may seem, both schools of thought are on board with one underlying premise that will drive the rest of this book: Work is human. And for organizations to thrive, love—the most powerful force on the planet—is the overlooked machine that powers teams and whole organizations to outperform the competition.

Still, in the minds of skeptics, and there are many, this four-letter word has no place in the harsh and cold conditions of the business world. Furthermore, in their minds, the very idea is disturbing as it sets a precedent for unwanted behaviors, norms, and rituals you don't want in the way of producing results or establishing a positive corporate image or brand.

Ah, yes. Perceptions differ, and people will run into all kinds of conclusions. Therefore, it is necessary to build some parameters around the word "love" to place the appropriate meaning of the word under the right context—in this case, a business context.

Love as a Business Strategy

As is the case, the word love is rarely mentioned in the context of work. It's off-putting, soft, and—plain and simple—just too taboo for the business world. Sure, we may love our work, and we may love our co-workers and customers. Still, we rarely think of "love" as an effective leadership or management strategy because, as stated, the business world wrongly assumes love as an emotion rather than as an action.

A quick refresher of the Greek language is necessary before we move forward (I also expand on this in the next chapter). Some of us remember from high school or college lessons that the Greeks referred to several types of love, yet only one truly counts for effective leadership in the 21st century.

Unlike *eros* (the romantic or sexual love that inappropriately shows up in the workplace and makes HR people nervous), *philia* (the quid pro quo love of "I'll scratch your back, you scratch mine"), and *storge* (the familial love for parents, siblings, or your children), *agape* love is your winner and what defines great leaders. It's the type of selfless "I got your back" love that demonstrates commitment, loyalty, respect, care, and high regard for others.

It is love demonstrated as a verb, not an adjective; it's backed by action, not expressed through feelings, emotions, friendship, romance, or charity. There's no such thing as the feeling or the emotion of agape, because it does not exist without action. As a leader, agape declares, "I value you as an employee and human being and will do everything I can to set you up for success so we can all thrive together as a team and organization." This is how the best leaders show up with their employees today in a way that produces action and results.

The Love in Action Framework

In investigating how best to connect agape to what science has discovered as its best tenets for leadership effectiveness, I needed a framework for application. I found one embedded in a letter written by Paul of Tarsus (the Apostle Paul) to the Corinthian church in the 1st century (see 1 Corinthians 13:4–7). Corinth, located roughly 50 miles west of Athens, Greece, was at that time a rich, unruly, and immoral city whose citizens lived a wild and unrestrained lifestyle. His letter to the church at Corinth was a problem-solving letter that addressed many organizational issues stemming from a lack of leadership we see in the workplace today: conflict, rebellion, lawsuits, confusion, disrespect, selfishness, gossip, pride, jealousy, a lack of discipline, and the list goes on. It didn't matter what the needs of the people were; everybody was out for himself. At this point, Paul points out to the church that the only way they will operate effectively is through love. He then presents a list of guiding principles for the world to witness what real love looks like in practice.

As I carefully inspected each stated love principle (action), I referenced it against the literature to solidify the case for business application. To my amazement, each one checked out in reputable studies on emotional intelligence, leadership, and positive organizational psychology. In essence, whether you're religious, areligious, agnostic, or atheist, you can say that science has finally caught up to what world religions have known for thousands of years. The principles from Paul's letter have been reinterpreted as a business philosophy that won't compromise results, profits, and excellence. They are as follows:

- Patience
- Kindness
- Humility
- Advocacy
- Trustworthiness

Examining the Evidence

In examining the evidence, I have uncovered the best available data, case studies, and best-in-class leadership behaviors and practices from personal interviews and conversations with the world's top leaders and leadership thinkers. In Chapters 3 to 7, I illustrate precisely how choosing the higher road of Love in Action, as presented in the five distinct actions, leads to a clear advantage.

Throughout this book, you will also find "Self-Discovery Pitstops" and "Leadership Toolboxes" to engage your mind and increase your learning. Don't let these exercises pass you by without participating, as they have been carefully chosen and woven into the chapters to amplify your awareness and improve your leadership. Also important is for you to note the "Action Plan" section that concludes each Love in Action chapter (the framework found in Chapters 3 to 7). Readers will be provided with action items they can immediately apply in their roles and organizations.

As we explore the era of remote and hybrid work environments and dive deeper into the digital age, it's evident that the workplace has drastically changed, and that leadership thinking continues to evolve. But what will never change is that humans are wired biologically to connect relationally and to feel and experience that they matter and that what they do matters. To that end, the Love in Action framework we will uncover will ensure that companies and organizations have proper guardrails directing them to meet their employees' greatest human needs.

Whether you accept what's coming or not, deep down, effective leadership is love practically demonstrated. To achieve business success and leave a legacy, the best understand that they must master their people skills. Indeed, it is a lifelong journey—a deeply rewarding one that requires immense courage and continuous learning and growth.

Ready to explore?

PART 1

The Question of Love

CHAPTER 1

A Shift Toward Sustainable Change

When you love, you wish to do things for. You wish to sacrifice for. You wish to serve.

—Ernest Hemingway

Ellen DeGeneres has been celebrated as a pioneer in the entertainment industry for years and is known globally for her comedic abilities and philanthropy. In 2020, revelations about the toxic work culture that pervaded *The Ellen DeGeneres Show* shed light on a darker side of her empire. In one investigation of the show's management, former employees came forward, exposing a workplace environment marred by allegations of bullying, sexual harassment, and fear. Many claimed that complaints against those in power positions were mishandled or dismissed, leaving victims without the support and justice they deserved. The allegations brought into question the show's commitment to creating a safe and respectful work environment for its employees.[1]

This is just one high-profile example of a work culture gone wrong. Away from the glitz and glamour of a hit television show, toxic work cultures in small businesses, hospitals, restaurants, hotels, manufacturing floors, warehouses, and expensive offices in towering buildings occupied by Fortune 500 companies remain prevalent and, to some extent, to be expected.

The year 2021 witnessed an unprecedented surge in employees leaving their jobs—over 24 million Americans alone between April and September.[2] This phenomenon, known as the Great Resignation, left business leaders grappling to understand the underlying reasons behind this mass exodus.

Despite much media attention focusing on employee dissatisfaction with wages, one analysis using 34 million online employee profiles ranked compensation 16th among all factors in terms of predicting turnover.[3] The reality? A toxic work culture was found to be 10.4 times greater than compensation in predicting a company's attrition rate relative to its industry average.[4] The crucial takeaway is that toxicity in the workplace represents the primary factor driving employees to leave during the Great Resignation.

Toxic work cultures don't happen overnight. They develop due to various factors and dynamics within an organization. Clearly, the best explanation for this is poor leadership. When leaders lack empathy, fail to communicate clearly, or prioritize their own interests over the well-being of their employees, it can lead to a toxic environment. When leaders fail to provide information about decisions, it can create a culture of secrecy, rumors, and mistrust among employees. Encouraging excessive competition without promoting collaboration and teamwork can also create an environment where employees undermine each other, engage in backstabbing behaviors, and prioritize personal success over the success of the organization. And when workplace bullying, harassment, or discrimination are tolerated or ignored by management, employees feel unsafe, undervalued, and unsupported.

The Consequences of Toxic Workplaces

As businesses continue to practice under these conditions, stories will continue to unfold about the damaging effects of uncivil and inhumane work environments on people's quality of life and health. Toxic workplaces are killing us—literally.

Swedish researchers at the Stress Institute at Stockholm University studied more than 3,100 men over a 10-year period in typical work settings. They found that workers' risks for angina, heart attack, and death rose for those who worked for toxic bosses. The men in the study, 19 to 70 years of age, had their hearts checked at work between 1992 and 1995. During the follow-up period, there were 74 cases of fatal and nonfatal heart attacks or angina (chest pains) or death from heart disease. The managers deemed the worst, increased their employees' heart disease risk by 25 percent. And the problems were found to be cumulative: The longer the employees worked for problematic managers in highly stressful conditions, the worse the effects. People who had worked for a poor boss for more than four years had a 64 percent higher risk of heart disease. These negative effects affected everyone, regardless of other risk factors, including how much they smoked or drank and regardless of their social status or income level. The study's lead scientist said, "For all those who work under managers who they perceive behave strangely, or in any way they don't understand, and they feel stressed, the study confirms this develops into a health risk."[5]

The researchers found that employees with managers with the following four negative traits were 60 percent more likely to have suffered a heart attack or other life-threatening cardiac condition.

- **Managers who were incompetent**. This may be the boss who was promoted too soon or was hired carelessly and who holds a position that is beyond his capabilities. Even worse is that the people reporting to this boss may be senior-level and have the expertise that they lack. Researchers found that employees who rated their boss's leadership skills less competent experienced a higher risk for heart disease.

- **Managers who were inconsiderate**. When bosses treat people like crap, it destroys their focus and motivation; consequently, people are three times less likely to contribute at a high level. The Swedish researchers recommended interventions such as delegating authority to employees and supporting employees' development to honor and dignify their contributions.

- **Managers who were secretive**. When answered in the negative in the study's 10-question survey, the statement, "My boss gives me the information I need," was most predictive of cardiovascular risk due to bad managers. This is indicative of the controlling boss who hoards or withholds information and ends up with employees who feel lost and confused. The Swedish researchers recommended interventions such as providing employees with information, giving employees sufficient control and power (ownership) in relation to responsibilities, and including employees in decision making.

- **Managers who were uncommunicative**. A failure on the part of managers who don't provide clear and realistic goals and expectations for people's work is another predictor of increased risk for heart disease in employees. The interventions recommended for improving communication include setting clear work objectives and providing ongoing and frequent feedback.[6]

Clearly, enhancing managers' skills by building their capacity to do these four things well, will drastically reduce the dangerous effects of stress on employees and help enhance the health and well-being in the workplace—and of the workplace. This is good for both human beings and their respective employers.

An even more alarming scientific meta-analysis of 228 studies to determine the causes that lead to death at work found 10 common sources of workplace stress destroying the health of U.S. workers:

- No health insurance
- Exposure to shift work
- Long hours/overtime
- Job insecurity
- Work–family conflict
- Low job control
- High job demands
- Low social support at work
- Organizational injustice

Researchers found that roughly 120,000 excess deaths per year can be attributed to these 10 workplace conditions, making the workplace the fifth leading cause of death in the United States—higher than deaths resulting from Alzheimer's, diabetes, or kidney disease. Researchers also note that approximately 5 to 8 percent of annual health care costs can be associated with how U.S. companies manage their employees.[7]

While modern workplaces have dramatically lowered physical accidents and safety issues, Stanford business professor Jeffrey Pfeffer, one of the lead researchers in the study, who documented the findings in his bestselling book, *Dying for a Paycheck*, argues that the health impacts of social- or stress-related work conditions have remained unaddressed. He says, "We focused on the physical environment, and we now need to focus on the social environment—the human environment."[8]

Pfeffer argues that typical wellness programs, which emphasize health risk assessments, exercise, and smoking cessation, don't work to prevent these outcomes. In fact, many times, workers will adopt unhealthy lifestyle habits, such as overeating, because of the overbearing and stressful work conditions they're in, which renders wellness programs useless because they focus not on prevention but on reacting to the harmful effects of what's going on in the workplace. In Pfeffer's words, rather than causing an employee to oversmoke, overdrink, overeat, and underexercise because of the stress they suffer in the workplace and then offering them a wellness program, employers should put the focus on changing the real root of the problem: overbearing work conditions and toxic management styles. Pfeffer says, "If I change the workplace so you didn't do that stuff in the first place, you wouldn't need a wellness program."[9]

In *Dying for a Paycheck*, Pfeffer smacks us upside the head with numbing statistics of the damaging physical and psychological effects of stress due to the workplace. A few among them:

- Sixty-one percent of employees said that workplace stress had made them sick.
- Seven percent said they had actually been hospitalized for workplace stress.
- Fifty percent had missed time at work because of stress.
- People routinely quit their jobs because of stress.
- In China, 1 million people a year might be dying from overwork.

This is the reason Bob Chapman, CEO of Barry-Wehmiller, one of the most caring and compassionate companies exhibiting love anywhere in the world, can boldly stand in front of a thousand other CEOs and declare, "You are the cause of the health care crisis."[10] Chapman calls for a human revolution while most senior leaders remain stuck in the industrial revolution of their minds. When we aspire to this greater calling of leading with love, in the words of Chapman, "It is about bringing our deepest sense of right, authentic caring, and highest ideals to business. It is about achieving success beyond success, measured in the flourishing of human lives."[11]

Holding up the torch and rallying leaders to put people ahead of profits is much easier said than done. Putting this practice into place in a real-life work setting can be difficult. To be fair, well-meaning executives are faced with untold daily pressures to perform financially that most of us can't imagine, whether it's pressure from Wall Street or the political pressures inside their own walls.

How We Arrived Here

At what point did people in positions of influence begin to exercise power over others to their detriment and manipulate people simply for selfish ambition? The answer to that question requires a quick history lesson.

When we look back at the values ushered in during the Industrial Age, we can see that using people in assembly lines for the mass production of goods was designed purely to make a profit at the expense of people. Although that era did boost local economies and raise the standard of living for most, and although companies did eventually introduce vacation time and benefits to keep up with market demands for competition, the powerbrokers who drove that era ultimately did little to benefit human beings from a human development standpoint. The focus and intent were on wealth creation and making products as quickly and efficiently as possible in order to benefit companies first and customers second—and not the people making the products. This workplace power paradigm (hierarchy), introduced as early as the 18th century, was based on power and control and the belief people needed to be incented or punished to get them to work hard.

Shareholders entered the picture in the latter part of the 20th century, and the heart of businesses turned to emphasize shareholder wealth creation. CEOs wielding power began receiving exorbitant salaries, bonuses, and stock options, and the era of greed and personal wealth generation became the primary motive for executives who bought into the narrative that rising stock prices raised your bank account by tens and even hundreds of millions of dollars. When money enters the picture as the centerpiece of why a business operates, the needs of the people move further away from the core of a leader's thoughts and aspirations. That's not exactly a recipe for love at work.

Milton Friedman's foundational writings on the purpose of a business back in the 1970s added fuel to the fire. Friedman, a champion of free enterprise, was enormously influential in terms of changing managerial mindsets and the educational material taught in business schools. His doctrine of shareholder primacy—squeezing every drop of profits out of the business and handing them off to shareholders—remains as polarizing today as it was over five decades ago. Friedman brought forth a provocative new phase in the American economy where "Greed is Good," and the one and only true purpose of a business was to make profit.[12] The way most Western businesses operate today can be traced back to Friedman's essays. In turn, love and care as progressive business values remain as distant to Friedman's model as Pluto is to planet Earth.

Creating Value for All Stakeholders

There is good news, though. A recent shift away from Friedman's model appears to be evolving. When I read the news, I was pleasantly surprised and even a bit shocked. The Business Roundtable, a nonprofit group founded in 1972 whose members are CEOs and founders at some of the largest companies in the world, including Jeff Bezos; formerly of Amazon, Tim Cook of Apple; and Doug McMillon of Walmart, published a document in 2019 titled *Statement on the Purpose of a Corporation*. The Roundtable explains, "While each of our individual companies serves its own corporate purpose, we share a fundamental commitment to all of our stakeholders. Americans deserve an economy that allows each person to succeed through hard work and creativity and to lead a life of meaning and dignity."[13]

Let's not forget that Roundtable companies employ upward of 15 million people and pay almost $300 billion in shareholder dividends, putting shareholder value first, above their own employees.

Although Roundtable members agree that shareholders are still important, the good news is that they also agree that corporations have a bigger responsibility to serve employees, customers, suppliers, and society itself.

I commend the efforts of the Business Roundtable, but the 2019 statement is just the beginning. Moving from words to meaningful change will take a decade or longer.

Everything rises and falls on leadership. To help this new vision materialize into sustainable practice that flows down to the frontlines, a change of the leadership guard will have to take place. We will need to completely overhaul our selection process to identify, hire, and promote leaders and potential leaders who embody the principles of Love in Action, which we will discover in the rest of this book.

Love and Profit

The story we must tell ourselves to shift our collective conscience is to believe in the real possibility that putting people ahead of profits actually leads to more profit. G. James Lemoine, assistant professor in the organization and HR department of the School of Management at the University at Buffalo, has done extensive research on leadership ethics and morality. He reminded me that people who don't think that love and concern for others are important for leadership will be reluctant to accept statements to the contrary and will be skeptical of the appropriateness or value of such concerns. Fair enough. Like Lemoine, my own experience as an executive coach and consultant providing training for leaders is that the best persuader for leading with love and care has nothing to do with the "fluffy" stuff and more to do with hard numbers and financial metrics. Lemoine shared with me that "there's a great deal of research evidence suggesting that companies and managers that prioritize active ethics and concern for others outperform companies and managers who are only laser-focused on profitability."[*] His key point is that companies

---

[*] Interview with Lemoine.

can increase their revenues and profit and be more effective by "focusing less on profit and goal-attainment, and more on broad stakeholder service, which of course includes followers."[†]

Take, for example, the practice of servant leadership. In past research, the companies made famous by Jim Collin's seminal classic, *Good to Great*, were compared to companies that applied servant leadership principles and a broader stakeholder focus. The research was based on the metrics that Collins used to evaluate the financial performance of his 11 publicly traded "good to great" companies: Fannie Mae, Circuit City, Nucor, Kroger, Walgreens, Wells Fargo, Altria Group, Gillette, Pitney Bowes, Kimberly Clark, and Abbott Laboratories. Those companies were then compared to 11 publicly traded companies that were cited in the literature at the time as having servant leadership cultures: Toro Company, Southwest Airlines, Starbucks, AFLAC, Men's Wearhouse, Synovus Financial, Herman Miller, ServiceMasters, Marriott International, FedEx, and Medtronic. The comparison focused on a 10-year period ending in 2005. Researchers found that during those years, stocks from the 500 largest public companies (i.e., Standard & Poors 500) averaged a 10.8 percent pretax portfolio return. The 11 companies studied by Collins averaged a 17.5 percent return. However, the servant-led companies' returns averaged 24.2 percent! Servant-led companies, where love was clearly present up, down, and across organizational lines, were even "better than great."[14]

Six Shifts Required for Sustainable Change

Engaging in high-brow, 30,000-foot-level conversations about shifting away from the shareholder value model is a start, but we should never take the focus away from the people who do the work. They are the central characters and heroes in this grand storyline that we must remember and cherish. We must remember to engage in a greater conversation about what it takes to inspire people to do their best work so that companies profit and human lives flourish. We must remember that humans are inherently designed to be relational and

---

[†]Ibid.

experience positive emotions. In the workplace, it's no different. We long for connection with others in the pursuit of purposeful work that produces meaningful results. Until we abandon systemic managerial thinking anchored in the fossilized ideals of the industrial revolution, where autocrats hold control, power, and decisions at the top, we will hold back the workforce—our most valued employees—from reaching their fullest potential.

To break the cycle of long-held corporate ideologies that still hold power over us—over them—a good starting point requires six major shifts.

Shift #1: Unlearn What We Have Learned

The first thing is to unlearn what we have learned—belief systems that have carried over from generation to generation as workplace norms over the last two centuries. For example, as children, we were taught many things that formed our belief system growing up. We were told what we could and could not do, what friends we were allowed to play with, and which we were to avoid for our "safety." As working professionals and business leaders, for the most part, our current belief system keeps us safe too, but limits us from possibilities that may increase our success.

Here's what I'm getting at. The real enemy that limits us is entrenched between our ears; those self-defeating thoughts and beliefs hold us hostage and keep us from growing. Not challenging our existing worldview and why we believe what we believe will only limit our own potential; it will keep us from exploring answers to challenging questions and cultivating new beliefs with unabated curiosity.

This brings me to a classic movie reference by an iconic Star Wars character. In the movie *The Empire Strikes Back*, the Jedi Master Yoda challenges Luke Skywalker to shift his mindset from self-limiting thoughts to one of possibilities. Yoda said: "You must unlearn what you have learned."

This quote has triggered and provoked people's thinking for decades. Think about what it means for your own life and leadership. We must unlearn many things first—things we perceive to be true and assumptions we make that limit us. One way to challenge our world-views and beliefs is to test them. By not testing your belief system, it will own you and become your ruler because you never questioned it.

We've attained much knowledge from school, work, life experiences, the "school of hard knocks," or through modeling behavior. But the world continues to evolve; we are in a new social, economic, and technological era, yet many of us hang on to information, knowledge, and ideologies that hold no truth to power. For example, people in management roles have not discarded the carrot-and-stick ways of motivating their workers; or managing through fear and intimidation. So, I want you to ask yourself one question: *What else do I need to unlearn?*

I had to take the Yoda lesson 25 years ago and really look at myself in the mirror because I was losing good people in a previous management position; I realized I had little clue how to lead them effectively. I was using carrots and sticks and pushing people in a direction I only wanted to go without inspiring them to a higher purpose. I had to be willing to go down deep to explore old habits and behaviors below the surface that were no longer working for me. To put it more succinctly, I had to unlearn and subtract old behaviors, learn, and add new habits.

The reality is that new generations of workers are motivated by more intrinsic factors that we will cover in later chapters. With that said, my hope is that you will begin to unlearn certain *misbehaviors* that stifle the human spirit and, in return, learn new behaviors that make people feel like they're growing, like they're being supported, and like their work has meaning and purpose.

Shift #2: Stop Seeing People as Objects

Historically, and still true today, as we look at what the workplace has become, most organizations see people as objects or functions—a means to an end in a transaction. If that's how we continue to treat each other—like the only value someone has is how much they contribute to the bottom line—you can bet that our interaction will ultimately suffer long-term. Leaders must stop viewing people solely as profit-making "resources" for several compelling reasons:

1. **Intrinsic human value:** Treating people this way reduces individuals to expendable assets, neglecting their rights, well-being, and aspirations. People should not be seen as mere tools or resources to be exploited for personal gain or organizational objectives. Every individual possesses intrinsic worth and should be treated with dignity and respect. Recognizing the inherent value of individuals promotes a positive work culture that fosters trust, collaboration, and a sense of belonging.

2. **Employee engagement and productivity:** When people feel valued and respected, they become more engaged in their work. Leaders who recognize employees' worth and encourage their growth and well-being foster a sense of loyalty, commitment, and motivation. Engaged employees are likelier to invest their energy, creativity, and skills into their tasks, leading to increased productivity and organizational success.

3. **Collaboration and innovation:** Viewing people as mere functions in a transaction inhibits collaboration and stifles innovation. When individuals are treated as objects or cogs in a machine, they are less likely to contribute their unique perspectives, ideas, and talents. By fostering an environment that values individuality and diverse contributions, leaders can harness the collective intelligence of their teams and unlock innovation potential.

4. **Long-term success:** When leaders prioritize building meaningful connections with their employees, they create a foundation of trust and loyalty. This, in turn, leads to higher retention rates, better teamwork, improved customer satisfaction, and, ultimately, long-term organizational success.

5. **Employee well-being:** Seeing people as objects or functions can have detrimental effects on their mental, emotional, and physical well-being. Leaders who prioritize employee well-being by considering their holistic needs create a healthier work environment. This, in turn, fosters greater job satisfaction, reduces stress, and enhances overall employee happiness.

6. **Reputation and employer branding:** In today's interconnected world, organizations are increasingly judged not only by their products or services but also by their treatment of employees. Leaders who genuinely care for their employees and prioritize their well-being establish a positive reputation and attractive employer brand. This can attract top talent, enhance recruitment efforts, and strengthen the organization's overall image.

Shift #3: Redefine the Role of Manager

Think back to your career and the people challenges you have faced. Most of us have been in varying degrees of boss-to-subordinate relationships, reporting to managers with different experience levels, personality types, and ways of seeing the world. Those work relationships adversely affected many of us; we may have lost our jobs, health, or dignity. Or perhaps worse. And if you haven't, you're probably due for a run-in with a boss who leads with an iron fist. Fear remains a prevalent way of managing in the 21st century—often with unfortunate consequences (I'll expand on this in Shift #5). This is far from being the best way to lead human beings to give their best.

Here's the problem. The current management model and mindset were never about creating value in human beings doing the work. We need to change how we view the role of manager and reverse the ideas and stereotypes projected onto us by the media of what it means to be the boss and be large and in charge. If you consult your dictionary and look up some definitions of the word "manager," here's what you'll find: "Someone who controls all or part of a company and manipulates resources and expenditures."

Looking at this definition, two words have an immediate, negative impact: "controls" and "manipulates." To reinforce this current definition and what we should associate with the word "manager," you'll find these synonyms in the dictionary: "Controller," "big gun," "head honcho," and "zookeeper."

Here's what the dictionary says we should associate with the word "employee": "Cog," "desk jockey," and "working stiff." On a curious note, "working stiff" was first heard in the 1930s and used to describe your average person who works at a not-very-interesting or stimulating job and for wages that mean a paycheck-to-paycheck existence. That's your working stiff.

The dictionary associates the word "work" with these synonyms: "daily grind," "struggle," "pain," and "drudgery." Putting it all together with tongues firmly planted in cheek, we are working stiffs reporting to zookeepers going about our daily drudgery. And you wonder why people hate coming to work in the morning.

But in all seriousness, this is the reality for many people in the workplace. We've built our organizations around this idea that managers drive people like cattle and that employees are expendable parts. Eventually, we'll hate our work and our boss. It's only a matter of time because these are the experiences we have carried with us from job to job. These experiences, in most places of work, carry with them an immense amount of stress for employees.

In today's business climate, we must challenge our current worldview of who a manager is and what a manager does daily. One common denominator about management is still foreign for many: every interaction should foster productive and positive relationships that lead to results. Arriving at this place means unlearning and subtracting a few things here and learning and adding a few things there.

Shift #4: Change the Business Narrative (and Lingo)

So much of what constrains leading with love concerns the irresponsible use of power by those at the top. They are also the ones who control the business narrative. As we've already covered, most business leaders continue to believe that a business's purpose is only to make a profit, which is short-sighted thinking. Sure, making money is necessary for businesses to survive and thrive, just like I need oxygen to live. But a business's purpose must be more transcendent and contribute to making people and society better and healthier. Money, in the long run, thus becomes a by-product of higher aspiration.

This is what we need to teach our business schools whose curriculums indoctrinate students into the narrow, profit-only narrative. The other reason for this shift is that these old ideas are not debated. The study and the history of economic thought are taken as a given and for granted. It's *business as usual.*

Another reason to change the profit narrative is that profit-driven business leaders perched in their Ivory Towers don't want to be perceived as weak or soft in the public eye. They must keep their tough exteriors and appear indestructible for fear of getting run over and losing their power.

The business lingo also must change. It's common to come across violent and predatory business metaphors, often used without much thought. Moshe Engelberg, author of the game-changing book, *The Amare Wave,* explains that expressions such as "crush the competition," "capture customers," "exploit the market," and "make battle plans" have permeated the business landscape for decades.[15] Engelberg forces us to look inwardly and ask ourselves whether business truly needs to adopt a warlike mentality. Is using violence-laden, predatory, and warlike language in our work necessary? As leaders, we should pause and reflect on the impact of such language on our businesses and ourselves. Engelberg advocates for a more caring approach rather than perpetuating a hostile and combative environment where the goal is to overpower and dominate customers and competitors. We can cultivate a healthier business climate by recognizing that we can succeed by replacing violent and malicious language with words promoting empathy, cooperation, and understanding. Ultimately, treating customers, competitors, and partners respectfully and with dignity leads to more positive relationships and long-term success. Though it may be met with initial resistance, embracing compassionate communication is worth the effort. The benefits of creating a workplace that values empathy and caring extend beyond mere financial gains. Engelberg writes that it uplifts our companies, nurtures a positive atmosphere, and allows us to connect on a deeper level with our stakeholders.

Shift #5: Eliminate Toxic Fear

All fear is not bad. In fact, some fear is necessary to activate the extra gear we need to overcome adversity. Swimmer Michael Phelps, the most decorated Olympian of all, has talked about being terrified every time he got in the pool before a big race. While some people's fear response is to choke under extreme pressure, Phelps's fear and mental toughness drove him to fight harder and be one of the fastest human beings to ever move through water.

Fear can also work against us to the point that it commandeers our brains, rendering us temporary idiots. The amygdala, often called the "emotional brain," swiftly activates the body's emergency response mechanisms when we perceive potential danger. Unfortunately, things go wonky when the amygdala decides that, under duress, there is no time for any reason and logic, and action must be taken now. Before you know it, you are in a full-blown fight or flight response, and a flood of adrenaline and cortisol is gushing through your body, which has short-circuited any attempt to react to the danger appropriately. Welcome to your Amygdala Hijack.

As you'll recall, my Amygdala Hijack moment happened after I stepped out of the shower and fell face-first onto the bathroom tiles, unable to move from the waist down. Under toxic management, the intense fear and stress had been building up for months. My instinctive response was to flee from the source of my fear—a high-level project that felt like walking on a tightrope without a safety net.

At what point does fear become so extreme that it inhibits our ability to make rational choices? A thought-provoking concept is the notion of "EuFear," coined by Andrew Colin Beck. EuFear (*eu* being the Latin prefix for "good" or "positive") characterizes a unique emotional state where feelings of joy and fear harmoniously coexist.

Beck's EuFear model centers around the EuFear Scale, a spectrum encompassing a range of fear magnitudes within favorable experiences. This scale spans from a state of "No Fear" (1 on a scale of 1 to 10) to one of "Full Fear" (10 on the scale).[16] Beck's framework proposes that neither complete absence nor extreme abundance of fear is ideal. For instance, in an organization devoid of fear, employees might lack the motivation to take initiative and get stuff done. Or worse, perhaps other employees, completely unafraid of consequences, might act inappropriately or take heedless risks that cause the business harm.

Without consequences for inaction and no accountability measures in place, people often don't take risks or make the extra effort. Conversely, teams operating under perpetual full fear might encounter severe drops in performance. In full fear, team members fight and work in a panicked state, many in pressure-cooker settings under scrutinous bosses. There's a complete absence of creativity and flow. The amygdala's hijack process is in full gear. Furthermore, a constant bombardment of full fear can induce undesirable physical responses, such as heightened heart rate and reduced oxygen levels. Or, in my case, a collapsed lower back and work disability.

According to Beck's research, the ideal level for *functional fear* rests at 4 on a scale of 10. At this juncture on the continuum, individuals encounter positive, constructive fear that aids in maximizing performance. A leader's role is to keep an employee's fear level around 4 or 5, just enough to keep people engaged and motivated without experiencing fight, flight, or freeze.

Richard Sheridan, who wrote the foreword for this book, is the cofounder, CEO, and "Chief Storyteller" of Menlo Innovations, a software and IT consulting firm that has earned several awards for its workplace culture. He said that one of his biggest jobs as a leader is to "systematically pump fear out of the room."[17] Sheridan explains that the negative "full fear" motivational tactics managers picked up from their mentors and other role models must disappear so that people feel safe. "If they feel safe," says Sheridan, "then you start getting the things everybody wants from a learning organization: creativity, innovation, invention, imagination, human energy."[18]

Shift #6: Make It All About the People

In the normal course of a busy workday, we hop from meeting to meeting, write reports, put out fires, and have tunnel vision about strategy, profit margins, hiring, or downsizing. We worry about delivery and pleasing our customers; we focus solely on the results but forget the relationships. We forget the people. Poet and civil rights activist, the late Maya Angelou, said:

I've learned that people will forget what you said, people will forget what you did, but people will never forget how you made them feel.

Most of us remember our best bosses because of how they made us *feel* as employees, but most importantly, as human beings. It should come as no surprise that actionable love, shown in how employees are treated and cared for, has repeatedly been proven to raise performance, increase value and loyalty, and improve employee engagement. But rarely do scholars, thought leaders, or the media intentionally call out these building blocks of the best workplaces as firmly embedded in a foundation of love.

Until now.

CHAPTER 2

Love

The Cure for Toxic Workplaces

When a flower doesn't bloom, you fix the environment in which it grows, not the flower.

—Alexander Den Heijer

Everyone has a great boss story. Mine takes me back to 2005, a few months after I left the surreal, toxic hospital environment. I had accepted a director position at another hospital and reported to an executive. To this day, Bruce (whom I briefly mentioned in the introduction) is my favorite boss because of his penchant for leading with love. Let me give you some examples of what that practically looked like in a real work environment.

Instead of leveraging his influence and positional power for personal gain, self-promotion, or demands for special privileges, he made me *feel* like an equal and never took advantage of his executive title. Indeed, he was the most approachable boss I ever had. He allowed me the freedom and autonomy to make important decisions. He gave me the resources I needed to become a better leader. While he was still "the boss," I was much more satisfied and engaged in that job than at any other time during my corporate career. The big difference? Bruce never managed people from the top down; instead, he led from the bottom up. We operated by shared values we all agreed on—the principles guiding our decisions and actions on our daily journey. This is important to remember because, in my coaching work with CEOs, I have found that the most effective work cultures ensure that everyone—the CEO, management, team members, customers, everyone—is treated with values such as trust, respect, integrity, and dignity. To accomplish this, senior leaders must create a work culture where values—how people treat each other—are as important as achieving daily results.

With these components in place, a tremendous amount of energy, passion, and productivity was unleashed under Bruce's guidance. We had a higher level of commitment because we could see the relationship between the organization's direction and what we personally believed in and cared about. After all, we signed up for this when we joined the organization. Bruce communicated an image of the future that spoke to why we were doing the work and how our work contributed to the bigger picture. Because Bruce had real relationships with us built on two-way trust, he could share his power by serving our needs first. It wasn't about Bruce, and, in turn, employee loyalty was off the charts.

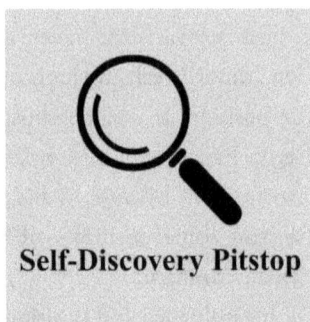

Self-Discovery Pitstop

Reflect on a previous (or current) leader you admire and answer the following questions. Use a notebook and record your answers, if helpful:
1. Of all the leaders you worked for, which one made the biggest difference in your life?
2. What did that person do that caused you to choose them as your answer?
3. How did that person make you feel?
When you complete this exercise, use it as a tool and measure of the kind of leadership that will inspire others, as your favorite boss did for you.

We have come to understand that feelings and emotions play a pivotal role in shaping human behavior. As a result, how leaders and organizations cultivate positive emotions within their workforce significantly impacts performance. Most of the qualities you wrote down in the previous exercise may appear like common sense, but they are not common practice in business. It's important to remember the second half of Maya Angelou's quote, "People will never forget how you made them feel." While Bruce and I never shared drinks at Happy Hour or developed a personal friendship outside of work, I felt the way I did because Bruce cared about me—loved me—for the better part of 8 hours a day, 40 hours a week.

The Cure

When we read about high-octane teams producing and collaborating at the speed of innovation, we see trust, respect, empathy, caring, and transparency as key "loving" behaviors that lead to high performance. Consider the hard evidence in some rather large, well-known organizations.

John Mackey, cofounder of Whole Foods Market and the company's CEO from its inception in 1980 until 2022, is an evangelist for love at work. He'll be the first to tell you that Whole Foods Market work teams are only as effective as the leaders who fully empower them to do their best work. This premise starts with building a foundation of trust, optimizing trust through transparent and authentic communication, and ensuring fairness for all involved. In other words, their leaders know how to love their workers. In a conversation with *Harvard Business Review,* Mackey eschewed the conventional thinking that "business has to be sort of ruthless and heartless to be successful."[1] Under his leadership, Mackey leveraged love as a business strategy, and it all started with the mindset of his leaders. He said, "The leadership must embody genuine love and care. This cannot be faked. If the leadership doesn't express love and care in their actions, then love and care will not flourish in the organization. As Gandhi said: 'We must be the change that we wish to see in the world.'"[2] Mackey calls leaders at the highest levels to stop being afraid and hiding expressions of love and care; instead, they should give themselves (and their managers) full permission for love to be openly displayed across the organization.

But how do we know that this strategy really works? Sure, Whole Foods Market is one company that seems to be having some success. Will it work for anyone else?

The Hard Evidence

Love sounds fluffy, but a surprisingly large amount of research deals with fluffy concepts.

In an integrative review of over 300 studies on ethical, authentic, and servant leadership, leader acts of morality and love are consistently related to outcomes such as performance, engagement, motivation, financials, and sales.[3] Turning to the research, managers who lead with a moral focus tend to perform at higher levels than those who don't. It's this focus that best captures love and care for people. Focusing on this approach has consistently shown to have strong effects on motivation and engagement. Unlike other leadership approaches, it also has unique effects in spreading concern to others. For instance, employees may go above and beyond for customers or prioritize the community.

Dispelling the Myths

Because the approach to leading with love is counterintuitive in today's command and control structures, skeptics have concerns and misconceptions, and I've heard them all. People do not understand love in action as a business strategy for performance and results. To them, it's too soft and weak. In reality, it is a far more daring and difficult path than people think. Some of the most common misconceptions out there that lead to objections include:

- **Leading with love implies having no authority:** It's a common myth that employees will take advantage of their leaders. The truth is just the opposite. Leaders who lead through love still lead with authority, but do so by supporting the employees while holding them accountable for success and high performance. As Bruce did with me, they demand excellence in others and can be tough. In the Love in Action model, leaders create a favorable environment for happy employees who deliver exceptional service to their happy customers. The whole organization succeeds.

- **Leading with love implies being a pushover:** This is a false myth. To effectively lead others through Love in Action, you must often do what is unpopular with the workforce or your team members. You may actually lose people at the crossroads of a major decision by taking a tough stand, sticking with your guns, and doing the right thing instead of caving to favoritism, popular opinion, or political pressure.

- **Leading with love is a religious concept not appropriate for business:** While the principles we discuss in this book exist across most major religions, the concepts of leading with love are universal and secular.

- **Leading with love implies a loss of respect:** A big myth that's been around for a long time in the business world is that leaders should keep their distance from their employees and elevate themselves above them in order to get respect. After all, if they congregate with staff members like peers, the myth goes, they'll begin treating the boss like a co-worker. You can still be the boss and direct the team while building solid working relationships that foster great collaboration. In the Love in Action model, a boss who encourages everyone to share ideas and thoughts and lets everyone feel comfortable speaking up, brilliant ideas pop up. You don't have to be drinking buddies with your subordinates, but the magic happens when bosses and employees develop trust and work together like a team.

The Greeks to the Rescue

Let's quickly refresh and expand on the Greek language, as discussed in the introduction, to dispel any further doubt and clear any confusion or misconceptions. The concept of "love" is so rich and intricate that the term in English doesn't fully capture its essence. This is why the clever Greeks developed eight words to better describe the diverse types of love we experience throughout our journey. You've got "Eros" for the passionate and steamy stuff, "Philia" for that buddy-buddy bond, and "Storge" for the family love that might involve a little sibling rivalry. "Pragma" embodies a love founded on duty, commitment, and practicality. "Ludus" is flirtatious and fun, without the strings that come with eros or pragma. And "Mania" is obsessive love, quite toxic, which is found in codependent relationships. So, what's left? "Agape" and "Philautia." As established earlier, only *Agape* love matters in this age of digital transformation and artificial intelligence (AI). Agape is unconditional love; it means wholeheartedly extending goodwill and genuine care to everyone with whom you collaborate. In human-centered workplaces that place people over profit (while *becoming* profitable in the long run), goodness always seeks the highest in others. When it spreads across an enterprise, Agape declares, "I value you as an employee, co-worker, and human being." It's the love demonstrated by Bruce in my favorite boss story. This leadership approach transcends mere altruism; as Bruce did for me, it's prioritizing the well-being of your employees and fostering a culture of care to cultivate a happier, more committed workforce.

But there's one hard prerequisite that comes before Agape Love. It's the last (but not least) Greek description of love.

Practicing Self-Love First

The Greek language calls it *Philautia*. Before truly loving others unconditionally, we must start by looking inward and practicing *self-love*. Contrary to misconceptions, self-love is not about arrogance, self-centeredness, or superiority but rather about embracing our strengths and weaknesses, building resilience, and accepting our limitations without shame.

Self-love is crucial for business leaders because it forms the foundation for success in all aspects of life. It empowers us to seek help without fear or hesitation, knowing that doing so only strengthens our leadership. Cultivating self-love is a personal journey that requires consciously investing in and consistently improving ourselves. Whether starting the day with 15 minutes of meditation, practicing gratitude with a journal, healing your traumas and triggers with counseling or therapy, going for a walk to reflect on your blessings and the goodness of those who have helped or inspired you, and finding practices that boost self-love is essential. But it starts with you and believing in your inherent goodness as a prerequisite for genuinely loving others.

Serve Yourself Before Serving Others

International speaker and author Robb Holman said it best when I interviewed him for my *Inc.* column: "One of the most valuable things I've learned is that you can only give what you got. If we effectively serve ourselves, we can effectively serve others in our sphere of influence."[4]

What are some examples of how leaders can serve themselves before serving others? Holman frames the approach around "integrated wholeness." It's ensuring that we have a genuine sense of who we are. In other words, to serve ourselves as an integrated whole, we need to discover or rediscover our personal purpose by understanding our core values, strengths, passions, and primary gifts. We need to be honest about our past hurt and brokenness, especially the need for having closure to unresolved trauma or conflict. We need to have a consistent and intentional time of self-reflection where we can be authentic about the help we need. This is self-love.

Holman expands further. He shared that we need to connect with at least one person in our life consistently and intentionally where there is no fear of judgment. This person acts as a source of encouragement, an attentive sounding board, and a practical voice of wisdom.

Ultimately, self-love—leading yourself first—is about personal stewardship. So many leaders today are stretched way too thin, running on fumes, and burned out without even knowing it. To be a good steward of your sphere of influence begins with taking proper care of yourself spiritually, emotionally, and physically.

Embracing healthy self-love grants you the confidence to make meaningful contributions to the world and the lives of others. By embracing self-love first, you improve your well-being and become more effective in leading and inspiring those around you. Loving yourself well prepares you to love others well.

It is important to acknowledge that self-love has both healthy and unhealthy aspects. Excessive self-love can create a sense of entitlement and narcissism and may result in aggressive and bullying behavior. On the other hand, inadequate self-love can lead to low self-confidence, feelings of worthlessness, self-harm tendencies, and other signs of poor self-esteem.

In her book *Love Is the Answer*, psychologist Fiona Beddoes-Jones, one of the world's very few PhDs in the areas of authenticity and authentic leadership, offers up a quick checklist (see the next Self-Discovery Pitstop) to approximate how much self-love you currently have in your life. As you go down the checklist, there is no right or wrong answer. Dr. Beddoes-Jones suggests that someone with healthy self-love and self-regard will score between 8 and 10 on the "yes" column. If there are statements you disagree with, it may indicate areas where you need to love yourself more.

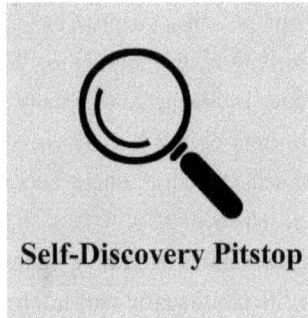

Self-Discovery Pitstop

Checklist for Healthy Self-Love Used by permission. © Dr. Fiona Beddoes-Jones			
		No	Yes
1.	I am worth something		
2.	My happiness matters		
3.	I respect myself		
4.	I expect other people to respect me		
5.	I accept myself for who I am and what I am		
6.	I avoid people who are very critical of me		

(Continued)

(*Continued*)

Checklist for Healthy Self-Love Used by permission. © Dr. Fiona Beddoes-Jones			
7.	I genuinely like myself		
8.	My thoughts and feelings matter		
9.	I am my own best friend		
10.	I am often kind to myself		

People who are really happy and successful undoubtedly have self-love in their lives. They also possess something else that is equally important for their leadership journey: self-awareness. Having the insight to understand when, how, or why we need to change to better ways of thinking and behaving doesn't always mean that we do. This is where the building up of one's self-awareness is so crucial for effective leadership.

Raising Your Self-Awareness

The previous checklist suggests a good starting point for developing healthy self-love. For the leader with a jump start in this department, the next step is having good self-awareness of one's abilities overall. It means defining one's present reality and then figuring out what leadership behaviors need to be learned and practiced.

Just as experience and expertise can often foster a misguided confidence in our abilities (we think we know more than we do), it can also lead to overconfidence in our self-awareness. A noteworthy study that collected data from 3,217 managers in 527 organizations, published in *Personnel Psychology*, discovered that seasoned managers were actually *less* accurate in evaluating their leadership effectiveness compared to their less-experienced counterparts.[5] This challenges the assumption that more experience always equates to a better understanding of one's performance.

In another study published in the *Consulting Psychology Journal Practice and Research*, researchers studied more than 3,600 leaders and found that higher level leaders tend to perceive their skills and behaviors more positively than how their subordinates perceive them.[6] These "blind spots" ranged from a lack of self-awareness about their communication styles and empathy, to their trustworthiness and decision-making approaches. Researchers noted that the discrepancy between self-assessment and how others perceive the leader could have significant implications for leadership performance, team dynamics, and organizational success. The underlying notion is that when leaders overestimate their performance, it is generally linked to traits like arrogance, which has been linked to leadership ineffectiveness. We'll be digging deeper into this topic in Chapter 5 when we unpack leadership humility.

Acknowledging and addressing your blind spots through self-awareness can bridge the gap between perception and reality in your leadership development. The key is to step back and evaluate what we know and don't know. Awareness of our limitations—one of many strong points of humility—helps us stay grounded and authentic. That goes a long way in winning the hearts and minds of the people under our care.

Measuring Your Self-Awareness

The Oxford English Dictionary defines self-awareness as "Conscious knowledge of one's own character and feelings." Researcher Anna Sutton further elaborates on this as "The extent to which people are consciously aware of their interactions or relationships with others and of their internal states."[7]

The most useful way to measure your self-awareness is to reflect and get insight into your situation and be open to understanding your own patterns of behavior that only other people can see. People who do well in increasing their self-awareness will score high in statements like:

- I often reflect on my thoughts and enjoy exploring my "inner self."
- I value opportunities to evaluate my behavior.
- I can usually sense the feelings of the people I interact with and understand their way of seeing things.

- It is important to understand why people behave in the way they do.
- I can generally predict how I will behave in a given situation.
- I am usually aware of my feelings and why I feel that way.
- When I fail at something, I usually can figure out what I did wrong.
- I am aware of the impact my actions have on those around me.

Reading over those statements, how would you assess your self-awareness? To go much deeper, in her research, Sutton developed the Self-Awareness Outcomes Questionnaire (SAOQ), a self-report questionnaire with 38 statements designed to assess the frequency with which you experience outcomes related to the development of self-awareness. This is a great tool for leaders and managers to explore positive changes and overcome difficulties (blind spots) they may encounter. You will find the SAOQ in Appendix A at the back of the book.

Is Leading With Love Tough Enough?

One of the biggest arguments against leading with love I hear is: *It sounds good in theory, but it's impractical in tough, male-dominated work environments.* But to suggest that it's impractical is the same as saying that honesty or integrity is nice in theory but impractical in the real world. So, let's look at two examples to address this concern.

I'm a big sports fan and love watching NFL football on Sundays. I admire the athleticism, grit, strength, and speed of world-class athletes clashing in the trenches of the gridiron. If you're still skeptical about the premise of leading with love being too "soft" and "squishy" for a business strategy, allow me to juxtapose this approach to the actual leadership approach of one of the toughest and most revered sports icons of all time: the legendary head coach of the Green Bay Packers, Vince Lombardi. A quote attributed to coach Lombardi found all over the internet goes like this:

I don't necessarily have to like my players and associates but as their leader I must love them. Love is loyalty, love is teamwork, love respects the dignity of the individual. This is the strength of any organization.

This is the same hard-driving Vince Lombardi who also made famous the statement that "Winning isn't everything—it's the only thing." We often view any notion of leading with love through the spiritual teachings of historical and religious figures such as Mahatma Gandhi, Martin Luther King, Jr., or Jesus of Nazareth. Perhaps long overdue, the no-nonsense Lombardi gives us a sober understanding of love and leadership to apply to today's toughest work environments. Surprisingly for his generation and even more surprising for the sport of football, this approach to coaching his players brought the Packers total dominance in the 1960s when they conquered five World Championships over a seven-year period (including the first two Super Bowl wins).

The grizzled and excitable Lombardi got the best out of his players by being tough-minded and tender-hearted; there was nothing sentimental about his leadership. It was a formula that worked well in one of the most violent sports in the world. Lombardi, the consummate player's coach, described mental toughness as "sacrifice, self-denial, dedication, fearlessness, and love."[8]

In the annals of military history, another example is the late General H. Norman Schwarzkopf, who stands tall as a compassionate leader with a profound love for his soldiers. Beyond his strategic brilliance and tactical acumen on the battlefield, his unwavering commitment to the well-being and success of his troops set him apart as an extraordinary military leader. The 6'3, 240-pound four-star general dubbed "Stormin' Norman" told Barbara Walters in an interview, "I've been scared in every war I've ever been in. Any man who doesn't cry scares me a little."[9] The General told *Insight* magazine that his first priority in the war was protecting the well-being of his troops: "I have loved soldiers since my first platoon, the first I ever commanded."[10] Throughout his service, Schwarzkopf earned his soldiers' heartfelt respect and loyalty, who knew that their leader genuinely cared about their personal growth and safety.

He prioritized listening to their concerns, understanding their individual needs, and creating an environment that fostered mutual support and cohesion.

The Link Between Employee Engagement and Love

"Employee engagement" is a necessary business concept that we are going to touch on throughout this book. But managers have yet to understand and fully grasp employee engagement as an everyday leadership practice. So, what does that term really mean? It can have so many definitions that even HR pros don't all agree on what it is. Many people talk about engagement like it's about making people happy. Companies try to force happiness with perks such as climbing walls, ping pong tables, free food, and massages. And you can bring your dog to work with you. During the height of the pandemic, many companies tried reinventing happiness in remote settings through virtual happy hours, virtual lunches, and virtual talent shows. These are all good things. They brought people together in a time when human connection was desperately needed. But none of that matters if the conditions required for employees to flourish on the job are absent. If the relationships at work are poor and the leadership culture stifles people rather than empowers people, you'll get low engagement.

Here's what it means: Employee engagement is an employee's emotional and intellectual commitment to the organization and its goals. Let me repeat that again. Engagement is the employee's emotional and intellectual commitment to the organization and its goals. And this is so important to leading with love because when we are emotionally and intellectually committed—when our hearts and minds are in the game—we give discretionary effort. It's about intrinsic motivation. It's much better than extrinsic motivators such as pay and perks, the carrot and stick way of motivating people. Why is this so important? Because if someone is paid a high salary but doesn't feel loved and cared for, they will still quit tomorrow or three months from now, regardless of pay and perks.

You want to increase the love output so employees are engaged, and the organization can release discretionary effort. When it's released, people will go above and beyond, go the extra mile, and do things beyond their regular responsibilities and job descriptions. An engaged sales rep will work just as hard making calls and setting appointments on a Friday afternoon as they would on a Monday morning. An engaged worker in a manufacturing environment will make fewer mistakes and have fewer accidents; in turn, safety ratings go up. An engaged nurse at your local hospital will show more compassion and better care for their patients, so patient satisfaction ratings go up. That's the outcome of leading with love.

Jim Clifton, chairman of Gallup, didn't mince words when he suggested that employee engagement is ultimately driven by a much deeper factor: "[Y]ou're going to find that what people really are seeking in return for work is love."[11] If anyone can back up Clifton's statement with scientific evidence, it is renowned University of North Carolina psychology professor Barbara Fredrickson. She has studied the science of human emotions extensively, concluding that love affects everything human beings "feel, think, do, and become."[12] Fredrickson, the author of *Love 2.0*, asserts that love is the "essential nutrient" the human body needs to thrive down to the cellular level. Whether you're developing a new app from your living room or surrounded by the buzz of brainstorming sessions in the office, positive connection with other human beings in a loving, nurturing environment is as necessary for us humans as sunlight, water, and good soil are for plants to thrive. "The more you experience it," writes Fredrickson, "the more you open up and grow, becoming wiser and more attuned, more resilient and effective, happier and healthier."[13]

Since positive emotions don't occur as frequently as we'd like, people at work need to experience more of them for longer periods of time in order for engagement to become more sustainable. "As eating one stalk of broccoli isn't enough to make us healthy, we need a steady diet of these momentary connections to have an impact. And given that people spend more time at work than anywhere else, their ability to thrive is really dependent on them having these moments on the job," states Fredrickson.[14]

Fredrickson's research confirms that employee engagement is established and sustained through Love in Action. She concludes,

> When people are made to feel cared for, nurtured, and growing, that will serve the organization well. Because those feelings drive commitment and loyalty just like it would in any relationship. If you feel uniquely seen, understood, valued, and appreciated, then that will hook you into being committed to that team, leader, and organization. This is how positive emotions work.[15]

This is also how many of coach Lombardi's players described having felt under his leadership, even decades after his death. It might work for your team members if it worked for hulking 285-pound linemen in the gridiron.

Is it time more companies embrace love as a leadership strategy to leverage business outcomes? Perhaps so, but this will require a monumental shift in our thinking. It's up to the rest of us to change the faulty perception that love in the workplace doesn't belong or its tenets can't be measured. For the general critics among us, we're talking about measuring the effectiveness of leaders in creating the conditions that will bring out the best in others through actionable love behaviors. Doing that consistently will be a game changer for improving every company's metrics for success. Starting with the next chapter, we begin to unpack the Love in Action framework that will produce extraordinary leaders.

Self-Discovery Pitstop

Imagine what great leadership looks like for yourself and reflect on it for this exercise. Write down your answers in journal form to the following questions, if helpful:

1. How do you envision making a positive difference in the lives of others? Go ahead and paint a picture of that. What does that look like for you?

2. What must you learn and apply to have someone choose you as a leader who made a positive difference in their life?

3. How would you like to make other people feel at work, as their leader?

PART 2

The 5 Leadership Principles of Love in Action

CHAPTER 3

Leadership Is Patient

I worry that business leaders are more interested in material gain than they are in having the patience to build up a strong organization, and a strong organization starts with caring for their people.

—John Wooden

We live in a society that values immediate gratification; we make hasty decisions and later regret them because we didn't think things through. We check social media several times an hour for likes and shares to validate our postings and comments. We feel frustrated waiting in line at the grocery store for a chatty cashier, and honk impatiently at drivers who don't move within seconds of a green light. At work, we negotiate for the things we need to get our work done to meet demanding deadlines and look good to our bosses. If we don't get replies to our urgent emails and texts at our convenience, the impatience meter rises, and so does our frustration level with others. A "what have you done for me lately?" mindset of more taking than giving has become culturally ingrained in all of us. We lack patience and demand things without much consideration for the needs and well-being of others.

In this chapter, we'll explore how patience is the foundational leadership trait that paves the way for a Love In Action culture. As we'll see, patience allows leaders to listen attentively. Patience gives individuals the time and space to learn, make mistakes, and improve without fear of judgment or repercussion. It's patience that allows leaders to encourage open dialogue and collective problem-solving. And it's patient leaders who avoid impulsive reactions and make well-informed decisions by carefully weighing all options.

Love Demonstrated Through Patience

We'll explore the power of patience as a key leadership trait that can drive impressive business results. But let's not overlook the flip side—impatience. It can trip us up, especially when it comes to managing people and organizations. We'll examine how impatience can lead to a lack of self-control, which can hurt relationships and decision making.

We will set the current state of management against the benchmark of patient leadership. This way, we can all work on refining our leadership skills and, ultimately, positively impacting the lives of those we lead.

To argue for leading effectively through patience, I have identified three business applications for individual, team, and organizational performance.

1. Use patience to slow down and improve decision making.
2. Use patience to improve organizational well-being and mental health.
3. Leverage active listening as a "patience strategy" to build strong relationships.

Let's get started.

Slow Down to Improve Decision Making

Patience is the companion of wisdom.

—Saint Augustine

Sarah (not her real name) is the CEO of a medium-sized firm known for her intelligence and sharp mind. She's also known for another, less favorable trait seen as a weakness in the eyes of her staff: impatience. One day, Sarah's team was tasked with a major project that required careful planning and collaboration among cross-functional teams. Despite the importance of allowing her team to work at their own pace, Sarah was constantly asking for updates every hour. While it's understandable that progress is important, Sarah's impatience created a stressful environment that didn't foster creativity or quality work. Instead of focusing on the task at hand, team members felt rushed to provide updates and keep up with Sarah's pace. Sadly, this led to mistakes and errors in the final product, inevitably decreasing morale and team spirit. Sarah's story is the reality for thousands of other leaders who demand results at the speed of hyper-innovation—on their often-unrealistic terms.

The Cost of Leading With Impatience

In high-pressure business environments, acting with a "sense of urgency" is often considered a necessary strength. As a headhunter in the 1990s, I worked in a cutthroat, 100 percent commission sales position, filling open work orders sent by Fortune 100 clients. Failing to sprint to the fax machine (remember those?) to quickly send a resume of a rock star candidate to a client meant losing out on a significant commission check, as my competitors (some of whom were co-workers sitting 10 ft from me) would be doing the same thing. Patience in such situations can be costly, as a lack of urgency means potentially losing out on opportunities.

Conventional business thinking further dictates that if you wait too long to gather more facts, pay attention to details, take more time to prepare for a meeting, or seek more feedback, the critical moment of a decision will slip away. In the Ivory Tower, the stakes are even higher: leaders have daunting pressures to meet the expectations of their boards, shareholders, the media, and the public, often making snap decisions that later prove ill-advised.

Let's flashback to 1986, which should have been a celebratory event for America's space program. If you're old enough, you'll recall watching the horrifying live footage of the Space Shuttle Challenger, 73 seconds into its flight, exploding into a thousand pieces under the clear Florida sky. Upon further inspection, this tragic event holds several lessons about the cost of leading *without* patience.

The project engineers at NASA had warned the people who called the shots about the "O-rings" that sealed the rocket boosters being a risk under cold temperatures. On January 28, the launch day, the launchpad temperature was 36°F. There were records showing that these O-rings had problems under icy conditions. One contractor recommended not launching below 53°, mirroring similar warnings of engineers and the manufacturer's own concerns. However, crucial information never flowed up the ranks. When it came time to decide if it was safe to launch, the top-level launch folks didn't know about the red flags others raised. There was a rush to meet deadlines, with the short-term goal of launching on time. The number of shortcuts taken compromised safety, ultimately leading to disaster and costing the lives of seven astronauts, including schoolteacher Christa McAuliffe.

In times of crisis, as we saw with COVID, it can feel like every situation is an emergency, and the choice to speed things up can actually lead to more chaos and confusion. One of the solutions is to step back and slow things down instead. When I work with my executive coaching clients struggling to balance their stakeholders' expectations, impatience often affects their leadership performance. I often tell them that it is imperative that they exercise patience and thoroughly contemplate their decisions with clarity and sound judgment before reacting when things are snowballing out of control. Unfortunately, patience is not common practice; a leader who processes tough decisions and is slow to impulse receives far less attention and acclaim than a charismatic boss with a commanding presence but a short fuse.

Go Slow to Go Fast

Dr. David Sluss, an executive educator at ESSEC Business School who has published compelling research on patience, defines it as "the propensity to act calmly in the face of frustration and adversity."[1]

Sluss reminded me in a podcast conversation that patience is active, not passive. It's acting calmly in the face of adversity, not *waiting* calmly. There's action behind it, but thoughtful, conscientious action. An example of this happened around the end of April 2020. Thousands of companies were locking down, but some hadn't fully moved to working from home. Sluss interviewed one such company, an engineering research firm, whose managers demonstrated patience by understanding each individual contributor dealing with personal hardship. While their work output and performance remained in place, managers allowed each team member to speak candidly, one-on-one, with them about their personal concerns. Exercising patience, managers allowed the reports struggling most with the drastic transition imposed by COVID to relax some deadlines and other constraints that aren't usually allowed to be relaxed. This more lenient approach to problem-solving helped boost mental health and ease the work–life integration challenges at the height of the pandemic.

This example runs counter to the blanket idea that patience means leaders must give in and give up and that business must slow down. In the case of COVID, managers who chose to respond with patience simply shifted by prioritizing the work that needed to be done. They looked at their business objectives and asked, "What do we need to do right now to keep us going strong in the face of adversity?" Their patience kept businesses driving, but the new motto became "go slow to go fast." The managers whom Sluss interviewed didn't relax all the deadlines. They weren't hanging back to get work done while the world went to hell in a handbasket. They showed up and went about their business steadily, as did their direct reports. Leading with patience meant they were still acting, engaging, and getting results, but they were doing them calmly in the face of adversity.

Slow is Smooth, and Smooth is Fast.

In Sluss's *Harvard Business Review* article summarizing his research, he used the example of the U.S. Navy SEALs, who live by the motto, "slow is smooth, and smooth is fast." Despite their need for rapid responses, these elite special forces teams approach their missions with a surprising degree of methodical patience in planning and execution. With over 60 years of experience in high-pressure situations, they've discovered that working deliberately and smoothly actually minimizes errors and the need for do-overs, ultimately accelerating the mission. Sluss wrote that leaders must understand the difference between operational speed (moving quickly) and strategic speed (reducing the time it takes to deliver value). This difference hinges on leaders clearly defining what "delivering value" means right from the outset.[2]

The leadership lesson here is that by taking your time to do things smoothly and efficiently, you are faster and more effective in the long run. It's a reminder that in the sometimes-chaotic world of a leader, maintaining composure and precision can lead to better outcomes. The SEALs' motto is not just about speed; it's about the smart and strategic use of time and effort. It's like saying, "don't mistake speed for recklessness; take it slow, do it right, and you'll find yourself moving at the speed of success."

Applying the motto, "slow is smooth, and smooth is fast," can have a profound impact on mental health in the workplace. Like high-stakes operations, the workplace has challenges, deadlines, and pressures. Rushing through tasks or pushing yourself too hard can lead to burnout and stress. By adopting a deliberate and thoughtful approach, leaders can create an environment that values mental well-being. Encouraging team members to take their time and ensuring a smooth workflow can contribute to a healthier workplace culture. It's a reminder that a calm and composed work environment fosters efficiency and mental resilience, allowing individuals to navigate challenges with a more precise and focused mindset.

Patience Improves Well-Being and Mental Health

Genius is eternal patience.

—Michelangelo

In a world where our brains constantly seek the next dopamine hit, becoming more self-aware of our actions or considering someone else's needs might seem out of sync. In numerous executive-level meetings I've encountered over the years, senior leaders of successful companies allow anxiety to be the driving force behind their interactions. Such an environment can be draining and exhausting for people. Worse still, it can spread from person to person until the entire organization is infected.

Impatience Spreads Like a Virus

Being an executive coach has given me a front-row seat to witness the rotten fruits of impatience. I've seen senior executives acting hastily and impulsively, which, down the line translates to middle managers making bad decisions, which affects relationships with people below their chain of command. The problem with one person's influence modeling impatience is that it's literally contagious. It's what psychologists call "emotional contagion."

Think of it like a social "infection" of feelings. It happens when one person's emotions and moods can spread to others around them. Imagine you walk into a room, and someone is really excited and happy; you might start feeling more upbeat too, even if you weren't feeling that way before. On the flip side, if someone is very stressed or anxious, you might start to feel a bit tense or worried, too.

This happens because we, as humans being, are wired to pick up on and mirror the emotions of those around us.[3] It's a bit like when you yawn, and someone else yawns, too. Emotions can be just as contagious.

Let's bring this closer to your own work experience. We've all had bad days at work, some worse than others. Next time you're feeling down, frustrated, anxious, or angry and have to lead a meeting on Zoom or Teams, your emotions will rub off on others and ultimately affect them. This can increase your team's stress and anxiety, ultimately decreasing their creativity and collaboration.[4] So, next time you come home and kick the dog or yell at the kids, it may be because you picked up someone else's grumpiness. The same can happen at work the next day, where someone else's impatience and bad mood can affect your day. You may be the dog about to get kicked, and the vicious cycle continues. We need a mental model, a skill, to help us break the chains of impatience.

Self-Regulation

The practice of patience isn't about changing what's happening around us, but about how we adapt to our environment. This takes the skill of self-regulation. Let me ask you a couple of questions: Do you take the time to think before you speak or act? Are you able to cope with things that are outside of your control?

Psychologists describe self-regulation as "reducing the frequency and intensity of strong impulses by managing stress load and recovery."[5] More plainly stated, it's the process of controlling one's thoughts, feelings, and actions to achieve a desired outcome. It's about swapping out unhelpful emotions for more constructive ones. The key to self-regulation is realizing that we have the power to influence how we perceive and react to situations around us. That takes skill!

For some, managing emotions is a foreign and fuzzy concept that can elicit an eye roll if that person's self-regulation skills are weak. Conversely, individuals with solid self-regulation skills can be more productive and better equipped to handle those unexpected nasty curveballs of life.

Business professors Debra Comer and Leslie Sekerka extensively reviewed the literature and found self-regulation to be the linchpin in developing patience. Specifically, they shed light on two potent techniques:[6]

1. **Situation selection:** This is taking steps to avoid putting oneself in situations that are likely to try one's patience. For example,

imagine you're aware that bumping into a particular colleague usually turns into a full-blown gossip session. You're not
interested in that drama, so what do you do? You take the scenic
route, bypassing their office altogether. This way, you dodge the
gossip train before it even leaves the station.

- o Now, think about a manager knee-deep in a complex task
  needing peace and quiet. They don't want to be constantly
  interrupted by folks dropping in with workplace grumbles.
  So, what's their move? They close the door. It clearly signals
  that they're in "do not disturb" mode, deterring unsolicited
  visits.
- o While situation selection is a powerful strategy, it's not a
  one-size-fits-all solution. It might not be feasible in some
  situations, like in a bustling open-plan office.

2. **Cognitive reappraisal:** The second technique from Comer and
Sekerka's study involves reframing the situation and allowing for
a more patient response.

- o Imagine this: You're all set for a meeting and on time.
  But the other person is fashionably late. Instead of getting
  annoyed, use that extra time to knock out other tasks
  or return some texts or emails. Reframe the situation by
  being prepared to flip the script when things don't go as
  planned. This prevents negative emotions from taking over
  and allows for productive activity. These techniques hold
  immense potential in bolstering one's patience.[7]
- o Let's say you're a newly appointed team lead at a tech
  start-up. The pressure's on, and you're keen to make your
  mark. There's a big project on the horizon, and deadlines
  are looming. Your previous self might've charged in, guns
  blazing, ready to show everyone how it's done. But with your
  patient leadership skills, you take a different approach.
- o You spend the first few days observing. You sit in on
  meetings, listen to your team's discussions, and get a feel
  for the dynamics. You resist the urge to swoop in with your

own solutions. Instead, you let ideas marinate and give your team members the space to voice their thoughts.

o   Then, something interesting happens. One of your quieter team members chimes in with an innovative idea. It's something you hadn't even considered, but it has the potential to revolutionize the project. You might've missed this golden nugget if you'd rushed in with your own plan.

o   By holding back and really tuning in, you not only let your team's creativity shine, but you also foster an environment of trust. Your colleagues see that you value their input and aren't just there to call the shots. Sometimes, the best move is to hang tight, soak in the situation, and let the magic happen organically.

So far, we've been exploring how to reframe situations and master our emotions to be better, patient leaders for those we serve. It's the self-leadership piece we must master first that guides us toward becoming influential leaders of people. By being more patient with them, we put ourselves in the position to minimize burnout and create workplaces that benefit our employees' mental health and well-being, which will attract the best people.

Granted, improving your self-regulation skills doesn't happen with a flip of the switch, but it can be done by learning and practicing specific habits to gain better control over your emotions and supercharge your productivity.

Patience Fuels Self-Control

With patience guiding the way, self-control steers you away from impulsive decisions and keeps you on course toward your goals. It's about reigning in those knee-jerk reactions and choosing thoughtful responses instead. When you're tempted to snap or react hastily, self-control swoops in and whispers, "Hold up, let's think this through."

While self-regulation is about managing your emotions, thoughts, and actions like a steady captain navigating rough seas, self-control is about saying "no" to immediate temptations or reactions, like passing on that extra slice of cake or resisting tailgating the car in front of you in retaliation for being cut off. Self-regulation keeps you composed and reflective, while self-control prevents impulsive decisions that make you a bit nutty. Both are vital to your mental health and well-being and how you lead others. However, there are instances when self-regulation needs a massive boost of self-control.

Leaders respond differently during a crisis. Some are rock solid, calm, clear-headed, optimistic, and a beacon of light for the team. Others react badly, throw temper tantrums, point fingers at other people, and act impulsively with more bad choices that send morale and productivity spiraling downward.

One of the significant obstacles stemming from a lack of self-control is unfiltered anger. I speak of bosses who express visible and public anger, yelling across hallways and conference rooms at the drop of a hat, or marching to other departments to "tell someone off" without realizing the fishbowl they work in (yes, people watch, take notes, and many are affected by it).

A very publicized incident involved Gary Friedman, the chairman and CEO of home furnishings retailer Restoration Hardware Holdings, Inc. In 2016, Friedman went off on his whole company with a flaming internal memo written mostly with the caps lock on. Unfortunately, his memo was "loud" enough to catch the attention of several in the media, and the story went viral.

In my own *Inc.* report on the incident,[8] the public rant pointed fingers at his customer service department because of an increase in canceled orders, which had climbed to 17 percent, up from 5 percent. But the threat of termination in the memo spared no one.

"YOU WILL NEVER GET IN TROUBLE FOR MAKING A DECISION TO DELIGHT OUR CUSTOMERS," Friedman wrote. "YOU WILL, HOWEVER, LOSE YOUR JOB IF YOU DON'T."

Anyone with a basic understanding of online etiquette knows that repeated use of all caps can be considered "shouting." As you dig deeper into this story, the angry memo was really a reaction to a bigger issue: Restoration Hardware Holdings Inc.'s declining sales and dismal stock value.

Friedman defended himself by calling his belittling of employees "empowering," and wrote "We have a leadership culture, not a follow-ship (sic) culture."

What Friedman missed entirely is that leadership implies follower-ship; you're not leading if no one is following, especially when jobs are being threatened by the CEO via internal memos.

Did Friedman's anger get the best of him, and did his rant go too far? Many agree it did. Friedman and others like him may have the best intentions to set direction, but they lack the patience and self-control to see things through other filters before pulling the anger trigger.

When Anger Goes Too Far

Let's face it: Anger is one powerful human emotion. It is also a very *normal* human emotion, so expressing it doesn't mean you're broken; it just needs to be expressed in a healthy, constructive way. There's a place and time for appropriate anger, and we all must learn how to manage it.

Stepping back and looking at root causes, you'll soon realize that your anger is a reaction to whatever is disturbing you, usually something unresolved at the bottom of your pile—feelings of anxiety, worry, fear of failure, humiliation, or powerlessness. Inappropriate displays like Friedman's can kill your culture, diminish trust, and send your employee engagement ratings spiraling downward. If mismanaged, it can be your worst enemy and sabotage your ability to lead well.

These are the primary emotions you need to deal with as you contemplate how to make payroll when cash isn't flowing. Anger is the secondary emotion that may lead to an explosive reaction. When anger comes knocking, and it will, we have to know how to deal with it appropriately so that it doesn't get the best of us. Author, educator, and radio preacher Chuck Swindoll said, "The longer I live the more convinced I become that life is 10 percent what happens to us and 90 percent how we respond to it."

Ancient wisdom says that "a person without self-control is like a house with its doors and windows knocked out."* You become

---

*Prov 25:28.

defenseless and open yourself up to harm. In a business sense, harm equals losing influence, respect, and the trust of those you lead.

The question behind self-control is: Can I manage my emotions and behavior to a positive outcome? Internationally known psychologist and best-selling author Daniel Goleman, says this about leaders with self-control:

> The ones who maintain control over their emotions
> are the people who can sustain safe, fair environments.
> In these settings, drama is very low and productivity
> is very high. Top performers flock to these
> organizations and are not apt to leave them.[9]

Respond Instead of Reacting

I've experienced my fair share of conflict in the workplace—some of it brought on by me. Since most leaders are in the people business, whether you work in close quarters to collaborate and innovate or are in a customer-facing role, self-control is a rather crucial skill to develop for success.

When things get hairy due to opposing personalities, larger-than-life egos, and a stressful environment at work, your buttons may be pushed. Leaders with high self-control respond instead of reacting (big difference!). As leaders, when we stomp on the war path to avenge ourselves against some real or perceived corporate wrongdoing and react with charged emotions, we are being impulsive, shortsighted, and usually not making decisions in our "right minds."

By reacting in the heat of the moment, we may end up clouding our thinking and judgment and escalate what should've been a manageable dispute into an all-out war with someone reacting back with equal or greater force. Bad move.

But by responding rather than reacting, we can step back, create space to consider the situation from all angles, and decide the best approach to handle things. That takes patience. It's the ability to process a situation about to go south, get perspective, and hold back from reacting head-on. It may mean making the decision to sit on your decision. You'll eventually arrive at another, saner conclusion by thinking over things rationally and level-headedly.

If you're still unconvinced, let's look at the benefits of patience.

Workplace Benefits

One clear benefit of patience is that it can enhance performance by making interpersonal interactions more agreeable. Don't read that to mean you're enabling a culture of weak people pleasers. On the contrary, according to research by business professors Christine Pearson and Christine Porath, when co-workers are patient with each other, they tend to treat each other with courtesy and sensitivity, making them more helpful and productive.[10] Moreover, being patient enough to acknowledge another person's needs and point of view can facilitate good teamwork in diverse organizations. The first step is being open to and inclusive of different perspectives. Teams and leaders of teams with different viewpoints tackle challenging problems and come up with helpful solutions.[11]

Taking the perspective of others is also key for boosting creativity. According to research by organizational psychologists Adam Grant and James Berry, when employees are fired up with a genuine desire to help others, it supercharges their own intrinsic motivation.[12] In three studies, they found that "prosocial motivation" strengthens the link between internal drive and creative thinking, and perspective-taking plays a vital role in this equation. As our work environments get more complex and fast-paced, research says that when employees step into each other's shoes, they're way more likely to come up with game-changing ideas that genuinely benefit everyone. So, not only does this approach ignite creativity for your teams, but it also gives us a deeper insight into what gets our people's motivational engines running when it comes to generating out-of-the-box solutions.

Don't underestimate creativity. You want to unleash it because it's one of the primary signs of an innovative workforce running on all cylinders. We still need the right leaders on the bus—patient leaders—to ensure that this is happening. Dr. David Sluss surveyed 578 full-time U.S. working professionals during the COVID-19 lockdown and found that leadership patience in a crisis significantly boosted their reports' creativity, collaboration, and productivity. When leaders showed patience (as indicated by employees' ratings in the highest quartile in his research), their employees' creativity and collaboration increased by an average of 16 percent, and their productivity by 13 percent.[13]

Hire More Patient Contributors

It may be time to consider making a case for hiring more patient individual contributors. Workers displaying patience ultimately could be the ones that keep a business from imploding due to people- and-leadership-related problems. In one study, researchers delved into the lives of 440 university students and discovered that patient folks tend to have higher levels of empathy, altruism, and discipline. With this mix of qualities, it's no wonder the researchers observed that patient individuals tend to handle situations and people around them with a greater sense of calm and grace, which works wonders in the pressure cooker environments of many workplaces. Moreover, individuals exhibiting patience were less likely to experience frequently changing emotions, feel anxious and tense, and withdraw from social interactions.[14] Do you think these traits would benefit your team or work environment when a project direction suddenly shifts? Or when you have to deliver bad news that affects their work?

In interpersonal work interactions, developing patience helps deal with annoying people with calmness and composure without getting too frustrated. And it's great for our mental health.

In 2007, a study was conducted by Fuller Theological Seminary professor Sarah A. Schnitker and UC Davis psychology professor Robert Emmons to examine the relationship between patience and emotional well-being. The study revealed that individuals who exhibit patience tend to experience less depression and negative emotions. This is possibly due to their ability to cope better with stressful or upsetting situations. Patient individuals also report being more mindful, feeling more grateful, more connected to society and the universe, and having a greater sense of abundance.[15]

Schnitker's study of almost 400 undergraduates found that those who display patience toward others tend to be more hopeful and fulfilled in their own lives. Moreover, in 2012 Schnitker invited 71 undergraduates to participate in a two-week patience training program, during which they were taught techniques for identifying their emotions and triggers, regulating their emotions, empathizing with others, and practicing meditation. Upon completion, participants reported feeling more patient toward the difficult people in their lives, experiencing less depression, and experiencing higher levels of positive emotions.

These findings suggest that cultivating patience may positively impact your workforce's emotional well-being and mental health. As such, it may be beneficial to promote the development of patience in individuals.

Promote More Leaders With Patience

We also want to place more patient leaders into roles directly impacting employee well-being, which the evidence strongly suggests. In one 2018 survey, 2248 employees from tech companies and household brands like Amazon, Apple, Google, Facebook, and Uber were asked to reveal which trait they find to be the worst in a boss. "Micromanager" was the No. 1 response overall. Not too far behind was "impatient."[16] Entry-level workers were even more put off by an impatient, micromanaging boss than any other grouping. Twenty percent of them agreed that their managers were "impatient."

In another comprehensive study, Deloitte Digital surveyed 2000 Gen Zers (individuals born between 1997 and 2012) and 600 bosses distributed across the other generations in the workforce—Millennials, Gen Xers, and Baby Boomers—to examine the working relationship between Gen Z employees and their bosses. Gen Zers were asked, "What characteristics are most important for a leader to demonstrate for you to relate to them?" Respondents were given 12 options to choose from: (a) Vulnerability; (b) patience; (c) transparency; (d) humor; (e) empathy; (f) availability; (g) broad history of experience; (h) similar background; (i) similar identity; (j) accepts my identity; (k) similar interests; and (l) similar political views. Respondents were asked to choose and rank 5 of the 12 options. Patience was the No. 1 most selected option, with 67 percent of respondents ranking it in their top five. Additionally, both Gen Z workers and their bosses agree with the understanding that the need for patience is important when cultivating working relationships.[17]

I was quite surprised by the results, so I reached out to one of the study's authors to better understand the data. It's worth noting that many recent Gen Z graduates had to start their careers in a virtual or hybrid work environment due to the pandemic. Many of these young professionals and their employers have struggled to adapt to the real-world workplace and the skills required to thrive in the years since. Jenna, a recently graduated customer experience agent, shared her experience of starting her first job. She mentioned that the training was mostly video-based, with little human interaction or skill-building opportunities. This lack of support and mentorship caused her to feel unprepared and isolated, leading to mental health issues. The Deloitte Digital data shows that Jenna's experience is not unique—only half of Gen Zers feel that they have been adequately trained to perform well in their jobs, and 59 percent of bosses share the same sentiment. Gen Zers and their bosses are on the same page when it comes to acknowledging the lack of preparedness.[18]

Simply put, Gen Zers worry that their performance post-COVID won't stand up to the challenge unless leaders thoughtfully create the conditions necessary for them to learn, grow, and succeed in their roles.[19]

Patient Listening Builds Better Relationships

I only wish I could find an institute that teaches people how to listen. Business people need to listen at least as much as they need to talk. Too many people fail to realize that real communication goes in both directions.

—Lee Iacocca

Active listeners have the capacity to pause and listen without judgment to someone they disagree with and hold back from reacting directly. People who actively listen are slow to get angry. So, their conduct is steady, rational, and manageable. In an escalating verbal exchange, they seek to understand first before being understood. And they speak little—giving them a clear edge in communicating and diffusing someone else's anger. Active listeners are those you can trust and depend on; these are the people you want to build a company culture around.

The human skill of active listening will be a difference-maker and the key to building strong relationships if you master it. With technology so dominant in our lives, we are becoming less opportunistic in developing our listening skills and less socially aware of the competitive advantage gained from listening.

Listening to Diffuse Conflict

When conflicts flare at your workplace, disappointment, fear, humiliation, anger, and betrayal are all bound to happen and are part of the politically charged corporate landscape. If you're ashamed to admit to yourself that you haven't exactly been the model example for managing your emotions when your emotions get triggered, join the club.

Conflict is unavoidable when human beings are involved, but how many of us have the courage to face it with tact and emotional intelligence? This is when patience shows its best features; people exhibiting patience understand how to navigate conflict for the team's betterment. They cut through conflict by listening and taking in various perspectives, asking questions to clarify both sides, and showing empathy to fully understand a situation before calling the shots. Using the skills of patience to manage a conflict provides a much faster solution to resolving a problem than running away from it. This is why patient listening skills are essential to master. It is simply the most natural and cost-free means to diffuse conflict and reestablish trust.

Unfortunately, active listening is not given enough importance as a leadership skill. Research suggests that most of us are poor and inefficient listeners; we only remember between 25 and 50 percent of what we hear.[20] That means when you talk to a direct report, colleague, or important customer for 10 minutes, you pay attention to less than half of the conversation. I'm certainly guilty of that myself.

When my clients in management positions realize the advantages of active listening as a crucial skill they must acquire, they often express surprise at how much they have been missing out on by not incorporating it into their daily routine earlier. But I also have to emphasize that active listening requires a receptive and nonjudgmental approach. Have you ever talked with someone who continuously interrupted you and argued over your point without letting you finish? This is not a conversation but a competition, where the goal is to win or put your opinion over the other person's. To truly listen, I tell my coaching clients that they must approach the conversation with an open mind and a willingness to understand the other person's point of view. That takes more patience than most of us are willing to give or able to do in the digital era. But it works.

Organizational Listening

James E. Rogers, Cinergy's former CEO and chairman (now part of Duke Energy) is a great example. He implemented a series of "listening sessions" where he met with groups of 90 to 100 managers for three-hour sessions. During these sessions, he encouraged participants to bring up any pressing issues. This approach allowed him to uncover valuable information that might have gone unnoticed. For instance, in one session, supervisors raised concerns about uneven compensation. Rogers reflects, "You know how long it would have taken for that to bubble up in the organization?" Thanks to these direct conversations, he instructed the HR department to find a solution promptly.[21]

This illustrates how genuine listening can lead to actionable insights and quicker solutions to organizational challenges. It's a powerful tool for any leader fostering a culture of open communication and problem-solving.

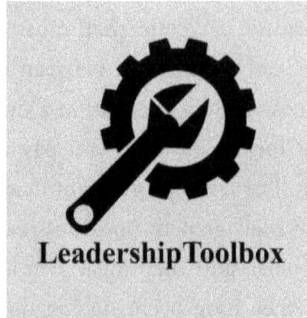

LeadershipToolbox

Seven Techniques to Develop Active Listening Skills

1. **Be Present**
   a. Whatever you're doing, stop and give the other person your full and undivided attention. What you're communicating nonverbally is, "I am interested in what you have to say."
2. **Listen to Understand First**
   a. During a conversation, most of us in influential positions tend to form a counter argument or point of view that aligns with our own perspective. Do not be distracted by the need to explain, defend, or fix. To break this cycle, just like when you put your car in park and it stops moving, park your own thoughts and try to understand what's happening with the other person.
3. **Be With the Silence**
   a. By practicing silence, you allow yourself to be comfortable with the unknown, stay in the background and in the moment, and let your true feelings emerge. Don't mistake silence for tension. If any tension exists, time perceptions get

distorted. Use "patient silence" to help the conversation flow naturally and both parties process things without pressure.

4. **Reflect**
   a. Avoid assuming that you have fully understood your colleague or employee's perspective and emotions. One way to ensure that you are on the same page is to reflect on what you heard by paraphrasing key points. This technique can help clarify any misunderstandings or miscommunications and show them that you are actively listening to them.

5. **Clarify**
   a. When faced with a conversation with the potential of escalating tension, diffuse it by asking the person for his or her help to clarify what's being said. For example: "I'd like to understand your problem better. Will you help me out?" This is about showing empathy to increase your understanding.

6. **Summarize**
   a. One effective way to ensure mutual understanding is to restate the key points discussed. This helps confirm your account of the other person's point of view and ensures that both parties are clear on their responsibilities and any necessary follow-up actions. Summarizing the key themes of a conversation can increase accountability and promote effective communication.

7. **Share Your Side**
   a. Remember, active listening is first about understanding the other person and then about being understood as the listener. As you gain a clearer understanding of the other person's point of view, you can introduce your ideas, feelings, and suggestions. From this point, the conversation can shift into problem-solving. Questions to consider: What hasn't been tried? What don't we know? What new approaches could be taken?

Deepening the Conversation

Active listening demands that you ask more questions to deepen the conversation. You want to keep asking questions because they allow you to probe and get to the root of the matter. Even after using all the listening techniques, you may still not have all the necessary information. In such cases, a trick to being an effective active listener is to probe the other person's feelings and opinions on the discussed topic. You can ask a simple question like, "Tell me how you feel about this?" and then express your statement about the current issue you want to explore. After that, pause, park your thoughts, and allow the other person to share.

One final thought on active listening: People generally listen better to other people who actively listen to them. In other words, someone at work will listen to you better if you are a more active and receptive listener when they are speaking. This will work to your advantage as a leader. We all want followers who listen and understand us. And followers want that, too.

As you move forward, approach your interactions with others with more curiosity and intentionality. Consider it a human experiment in your professional development journey, with active listening as a key tool in your toolbox.

Action Plan

It is widely accepted that those in top management positions significantly impact the organization's culture. When they demonstrate patience, it inspires others to develop this skill. With that in mind, here is a plan of action to help leaders establish a culture or team that values patience. It starts with them modeling the behaviors for others to follow.

Action Item 1: Identify Your Triggers

Create a list of places, events, and people that have tested your patience and where you need to exercise more patience. This journaling exercise can help leaders (and their employees) avoid trigger situations, develop and practice cognitive reappraisal techniques (reframing), and monitor their progress toward the goal of patience. Once you record your list of triggers, you can develop a strategy to handle impatient reactions.

⚲ Action Item 2: Reflect

1. **Focus your mind:** For 10 minutes, find a quiet spot, preferably first thing in the morning, away from noise, distractions, and children. Reflect on the positive things in your life and your purpose in the world. This small ritual will help you feel more in control throughout the day, and you'll notice a difference in the weight lifted off your shoulders.

2. **Have a gratitude ritual:** Cultivating gratitude can significantly reduce stress. Research in experimental psychology has shown that people who feel more grateful are better at delaying gratification and are more patient.[22]
   o   One way to cultivate gratitude is by jotting down small daily wins. Reflect on the good things in life for 60 seconds. Now open your eyes, and for the next 2 minutes, journal three things you are grateful for the previous day. Setting aside this little ritual makes the rest of your day seem manageable.

3. **Perform conscious breathing:** Beginning the day flustered can lead to a short fuse, causing a small problem to escalate into a bigger one. Psychologists discovered that "conscious breathing"—a focused form of yoga-based breathing meditation—can significantly reduce stress and anxiety levels—sometimes in minutes.[23]
   a.   For 5 minutes, take deep breaths with longer exhales than your inhales. Observe your breath going in and out. This helps your brain focus on one thing at a time; it can help you start your day with a calm, alert, and prepared mind, significantly enhancing your interactions with team members.

4. **Measure up:** When you're stuck in the decision-making process, use what researchers call the "measure up" method.[24] This is about taking a pause and reflecting about which option aligns best with the expectations of others and the high standards you've set for yourself. As part of your reflection process, find trusted sources and mentors and speak to them about your

current course of action. Then, process some more. Lastly, lean on your personal mottos and values forged from life experiences. Ask yourself, "What kind of mark do I want to leave on this world?" Next time you're wrestling with a decision, just remember to measure it against what truly matters to you and those around you.

Action Item 3: Slow Down

1. **Think before you act:** When times get stressful, rushing through things such as decision making or going over someone's head can be convenient. This can also potentially create an even bigger issue down the road. Instead, think critically but also emotionally with other people's consideration in mind so you can make the right call, not the easy one.

2. **Downshift:** Rather than race to the finish and focus solely on the results, when you finish a task, downshift your mind to a lower gear to resist the urge to get the next task or make the next decision in a perpetual state of urgency.

3. **Let your mind wander:** During a work meeting, instead of solely focusing on getting through the agenda, take the time to look around the room and pay attention. Observe if your co-workers seem engaged or disinterested, and if the conversation is headed in the right direction.

   a. One approach is mental meandering; let your thoughts, feelings, and attention wander for a few minutes to see where they go. Take a break from accomplishing tasks and look up from your computer screen.

   b. Another suggestion involves slowing down physically to slow down mentally. For instance, when holding meetings away from the office, leave early to make your way there slowly and get a feel for how things are going.

4. **Enjoy the moment:** We need to remember to enjoy the moment. Mindfulness, for example, is all about being present and immersed in the here and now. Here's a nifty trick to rewire

your brain: spend 15 minutes savoring your morning coffee while catching the morning sunrise. A little ritual like this can help you build up patience for those unexpected moments when things don't go as planned or take longer than expected.

Action Item 4: Practice Self-Control

1. **Get perspective:** The next time you get sucked into a conflict, assess the situation, listen to many voices without judgment, process the information, and hold back from reacting impulsively. Once you get full clarity, you can determine the proper course of action.
   a. At times, it means the decision to sit on your decision. Think over your situation rationally after hearing all sides, without getting sucked into the drama, and you'll eventually arrive at more rational conclusions.
2. **Take a six-second pause:** When things get saucy and insults are flying across the room, brain science can help you with a valuable technique: the six-second pause. Why six seconds? The chemicals of emotion inside our brains and bodies typically last for about six seconds. During a heated exchange, if we can pause briefly, the flood of chemicals being produced slows down. This pause helps you to quickly assess the costs and benefits of various actions before saying something nasty that you will later regret. After the six-second pause, you can respond more thoughtfully and constructively.
3. **Model positivity:** In severely impatient settings, negative emotions such as criticism and blaming are par for the course during a conflict. To rise above the suffocating dust that kicks up during a conflict, promote positive emotions that support big-picture thinking, brainstorming, and creativity. As you introduce positivity into future conversations and focus first on non-negative topics, you can train parties to "lay down their weapons," relax, actively listen, and patiently engage in respectful problem-solving.

Action Item 5: *Simplify Your Day*

Impatient people are often perfectionists and multitaskers, which is counterproductive and keeps them in constant anxiety and disarray. Spend 5 minutes answering the following questions to pare down your day:

1. What will grow you personally or professionally and improve you as a human being today?
2. What will excite you and give you more energy today?
3. What will set the stage for an epic-productive day?

Make sure you write down your answers before leaving for work, and more importantly, have them visible as reminders during the day. Staying on track to accomplish these energizing goals will elevate your mind to a positive state throughout the day.

CHAPTER 4

Leadership Is Kind

Be kind whenever possible. It is always possible.

—Dalai Lama

Kindness, like patience, is a rare commodity in business. It's often seen as a moral obligation that not everyone feels obliged to. There are several reasons why kindness is in short supply. One is the relentless pursuit of profit itself. In the race to the bottom line, where quarterly reports and aggressive financial metrics dominate C-suite discussions, the belief is that kindness wouldn't cut it in the cutthroat business world—it's too much of a luxury and, at times, a liability. In fact, you may be nodding your head in agreement. The focus on "cash is king" has overshadowed the importance of human connections, where kindness resides. In the end, as the Cuba Gooding Jr. character said in *Jerry Maguire*, "Show me the money!"

Another reason for the shortage of kindness is a lack of time. Everyone is so caught up in meetings, deadlines, and endless to-do lists that they scarcely have a moment to spare for a kind gesture. In this whirlwind of productivity, kindness is often forgotten.

But the real root cause for the shortage of kindness extends beyond the office. It includes the breakdown of social bonds, the widening political spectrum pushing people to extreme ideological views, racism, multiple wars, growing antisemitism, Islamophobia, transphobia, and a general unwillingness to care about others. When empathy and compassion evolved, we lived in close-knit tribes and had meaningful connections with almost everyone we interacted with, which gave us ample reasons to care for one another. It was an inherent part of life. Now, we often feel isolated, stressed, and surrounded by hostility. Society is a hot mess, but we must continue to model empathic behavior where we spend so much of our awake hours, one leader at a time, one team at a time, one company at a time. It's high time for the business world to be the "shining city on a hill" for the rest of the world to emulate.

Balancing the Scales

Most of us would agree that, in business, the scales tip heavily toward hard currency, spurred by aggressive financial targets, and not enough on the soft currency of kindness to elevate human potential and well-being. While the lopsidedness may yield short-term gains, the pressure to perform on the workforce often leads to burnout, decreased morale, and higher turnover rates.

This tenacious hunt for financial goals to meet the expectations of boards, shareholders, and soulless executives needs a counterweight. What if, by balancing this scale with the currency of kindness, we could achieve unprecedented human performance, eliminate burnout, decrease turnover, and achieve even better business outcomes? (See Figure 4.1.)

One previous company I worked for was known for its culture of hyperproductivity, but was drastically short on kindness. Employees worked long hours, and the pressure to meet aggressive performance goals was palpable. While the company saw some financial gains during my two-year tenure, the toll on employee well-being was significant. Eventually, burnout levels reached a breaking point, and the company experienced an astounding 60 percent turnover, which hurt its bottom line. Not long after, the business dissolved.

Still, we know that kindness goes against the grain of most transactional work environments. In today's stressful pressure cookers, where we see so much suffering (refer back to Chapter 1), we need kindness more than ever. My hope is that you will be convinced of the superpower effects of kindness to counteract burnout and boost morale and well-being.

Kindness Is Not "Nice"

But first, let's clarify kindness for workplace application. Too many of us have a formed picture of kindness as simply being a nice person. At

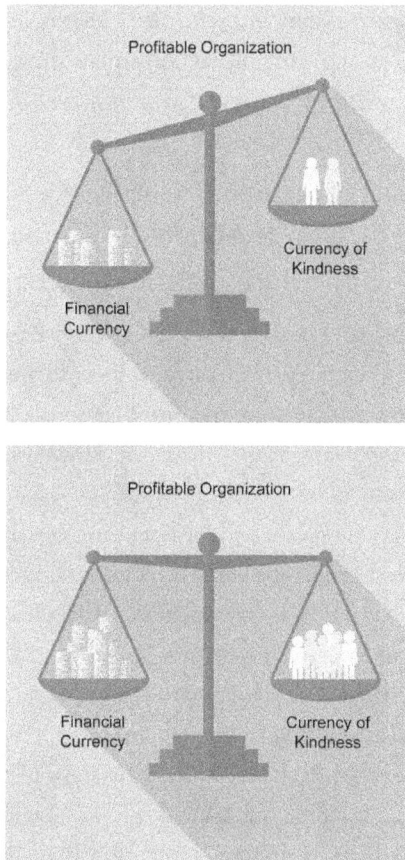

Figure 4.1 Illustrations (scales)

first glance, "nice" and "kind" may seem synonymous. After all, an act of kindness is nice, and being nice can be seen as a form of kindness. But the real difference between someone being nice and someone being kind often boils down to the intention behind the action.

Being nice is doing something pleasant or agreeable; it's that friendly pat on the back. We're conditioned to be nice to each other by holding the door open for someone. Niceness is the polite thing to do, and we're even lacking *that* these days!

But kindness is not just a surface-level action; it's a conscious choice. Kindness is a deeper well. It's about being selfless and showing benevolence—your humanity, your generosity, and your goodwill. In the Corinthians' account, the Greek root word for kindness (chrēsteuomai) means to be "useful, serving, and gracious." There's intent behind each word; it involves taking tangible actions that show you care about others. Kindness comes with a moral compass, too. Being kind is just the right thing to do in the moment.

The Chain Reaction of Kindness

In the summer of 2017, an eight-year-old boy and his eleven-year-old brother were enjoying a swim at Panama City Beach, Florida. But suddenly, a fierce rip current surged, carrying them further into the Gulf of Mexico. Their frantic cries reached their mother on the shore, who wasted no time and bravely swam out to their aid. However, the unforgiving current was too strong for her as well. Even their 67-year-old grandmother, showing remarkable courage, joined the rescue mission but suffered a heart attack in the process. Despite the efforts of other strangers who came to the rescue, the current's power was too much. Nine lives hung in the balance, with no lifeguards or emergency help in sight.

Yet, on that very shore, a young couple, Derek and Jessica Simmons, newly transplanted to Florida from Alabama, stepped up. They quickly rallied bystanders, urging them to link arms in a show of solidarity. "I come from a place where you help out your neighbor," Derek Simmons later explained. This call to action resonated, and more than 80 people united to form a human chain that stretched out into the water. In a heart-pounding hour, these strangers worked together, passing each exhausted swimmer along the chain and bringing them back to safety, one by one, including the grandmother, who later recovered from her heart attack.

After the rescue, Simmons described what he experienced: "It was pretty amazing, all these different people, complete strangers who didn't even know each other's names, hugging and high-fiving."[1]

As you read this account, please check in with yourself. How did you feel? Did you notice that gentle swell in your chest or maybe a lump forming in your throat? Maybe a sense of openness, joy, or relief as you soaked in the inspiring story? If so, kindness has already impacted your very soul. What you may have experienced is what psychologists call "elevation."[2] It's similar to awe or deep admiration and is triggered by witnessing someone demonstrate moral courage or perform a heroic act.

Elevation, however, is more than just getting the warm fuzzies from reading a feel-good story. It has a significant impact on our behavior when experienced in person. It sparks a strong urge to mirror the behavior we just witnessed, nudging us to be less self-centered and more helpful to those around us. When we see someone lend a hand at work, it inspires us to do the same, creating a chain reaction of kindness that inspires us to help others.

Research on elevation by Jonathan Haidt and colleagues found that when study participants witnessed acts of kindness and were later asked, "Did the feeling give you any inclination toward doing something?" the usual answer was a nod toward wanting to be more helpful and generous.[3]

Elevation pops up at work in everyday places such as factory floors, boardrooms, retail spaces, and corporate offices. In a study conducted in 2010, insights were gathered from the workforce regarding their feelings toward their bosses. The study revealed that leaders who demonstrated fairness (a topic explored in Chapter 6) and a willingness to put the team's interests before their own (a topic explored in Chapter 5) could spark a feeling of elevation in their followers. As a result, workers began to view their bosses in a positive light, leading to increased kindness and helpfulness toward colleagues and loyalty to the organization.[4]

The plain reality is that watching a peer or co-worker help another causes you to want to reciprocate. Since most individuals inherently desire to be part of a community where people treat each other with kindness and respect (more on that later), witnessing a boss or co-worker perform a small act of kindness for another can rekindle our hope that such a world is possible, so you're more likely to pay it forward.

As kindness spreads throughout the organization with co-workers helping each other out, a snowball effect takes place: The work atmosphere becomes more civil and less fear-based, and employees not only provide better customer service on their own accord, without prompting, but they also develop better relationships at work. Kindness begets kindness and spreads like wildfire. Imagine the possibilities of such a culture of work.

Empathetic Interactions

If there is any one secret of success, it lies in the ability to get the other person's point of view and see things from his angle as well as your own.

—Henry Ford

Gen-Z is one of the main drivers of change in today's workplace, making up nearly a quarter of the U.S. workforce. Many began their careers in a work landscape dramatically altered by the pandemic and have different needs and expectations than previous generations.

In Deloitte Digital's survey of 2,000 Gen-Zers referenced in Chapter 3, you will recall that both Gen-Zers and their bosses agree that patience is the most important characteristic that bosses can demonstrate. Gen-Zers list *empathy* as the second most important characteristic, while bosses rank empathy as a distant fifth. Further, only 35 percent of Gen-Zers feel that their boss is empathetic. Looking closer at the data, Gen-Zers who feel cared for at work are 3.3 times more likely to look forward to coming to work and are less likely to have plans to leave their job, so empathy is good for retention.

"Empathy plays a vital role in engaging Gen-Z workers who prioritize feeling valued and heard by their bosses," said Amelia Dunlop, chief experience officer at Deloitte Digital, who authored the study.[5]

Empathy Is Not Sympathy

The first step on our road to more empathetic leadership and workplaces is to distinguish it from sympathy. While empathy and sympathy are often used interchangeably, they are fundamentally different. Researcher and author Dr. Brené Brown offers one of the best explanations of these two concepts and why empathy is crucial. In a presentation to the Royal Society of Arts (RSA), Brown said, "Empathy fuels connection. Sympathy drives disconnection."[6]

Empathy fuels connection. Sympathy drives disconnection.

—Dr. Brené Brown

"Empathy is feeling with people," says Brown. It says, "I feel with you," not "for you," which is what sympathy does. When a stressed-out teammate is feeling the weight of a massive project and a looming deadline that could have serious consequences, the empathic response from a colleague is to let them know they're not going through this alone. The response here is to be listening and tell them they can lean on you to navigate this challenging time.

Note that empathy is a way to connect with another person's emotions; it doesn't require us to have experienced the same situation. When practiced skillfully, it's much more potent than the sympathetic platitude of "Bless your heart. I hope it works out for you."

Driving home Brown's point, when empathy reaches a leadership conversational skill displayed among teams, it helps bring people together. It fosters a sense of inclusivity, while sympathy can lead to further isolation despite coming from a good place. To put it another way, Brown explains that sympathy impedes empathy because it is the response we give "when we *don't* want to be vulnerable to someone else's struggle."[7]

Self-Discovery Pitstop

Ask yourself five questions to be more empathetic.
• Have I recognized and worked through my own fears and anxieties about change?
• Do I choose rational thought to avoid my emotional response?
• Am I comfortable verbally articulating my emotions to others?
• Am I able to manage my own emotions so that I can listen more intently to the emotions others are experiencing?
• Do I have what it takes to emotionally support my team through business transformation?

Conversational Superpower

According to Stanford professor Jamil Zaki (who calls empathy "a workplace superpower"), when bosses and organizations are perceived as empathetic, employees are more satisfied in their jobs and take more creative risks.[8] They are far less likely to report severe burnout or develop physical stress symptoms and are more resilient in the face of adversity.

They also tend not to quit: A 2022 Gallup survey of more than 15,000 U.S. employees found that those with caring employers were 69 percent less likely to actively search for a new job and 71 percent less likely to report experiencing a lot of burnout. Additionally, they were five times more likely to strongly advocate for their company as a place to work.[9]

And yet, let's be real. No leader can claim to be perfect because there is no perfect leader. However, it is in the interpersonal communication realm where human nature tends to falter and where we can improve our leadership skills. I've seen all kinds of people problems take place repeatedly with my clients (otherwise, I'd be out of business). On any given day, leaders and managers must deal with various personality types and navigate tricky scenarios affecting people's lives. The response to how you communicate and the words you choose can get messy due to the unpredictable nature of humanity. Therefore, it is essential to skillfully apply an empathetic style of interpersonal interaction, where and when appropriate, to ensure your success.

Expanding on this belief, global training giant Development Dimensions International (DDI) assessed over 15,000 leaders from more than 300 organizations across 20 industries and 18 countries to determine which conversational skills impact overall performance most.

The findings, published in their High-Resolution Leadership Report,[10] are revealing. While skills such as "encouraging involvement of others" and "recognizing accomplishments" are necessary and essential, listening and responding with empathy rose to the top as the most critical driver of overall performance. It also consistently relates to higher performance in decision making, coaching, engaging, and planning and organizing. As shown in Figure 4.2, the bigger the circle, the stronger the relationship between the interaction skill and job performance.

Unfortunately, only 40 percent of the frontline leaders DDI assessed were proficient or strong in empathy as an interaction skill.[11]

Getting Empathy Right

Leaders often feel compelled to provide solutions to problems, but when it comes to personal or emotional challenges faced by employees, it's smarter to generate empathy by giving them space to talk and feel heard. You also want to avoid giving automatic responses or one-size-fits-all advice. Every employee is different, and their problems require unique solutions.

The objective is to create an environment where employees feel comfortable sharing their concerns with you, knowing you are there to help them in any way you can. You show your empathy by being willing to listen, validating their feelings, and offering support whenever possible.

Even people who are traditionally dominated by left-brain thinking, challenged by interpersonal skills, and focused on data and details would agree that leading with empathy is a brilliant strategy. When you take on the perspective of those you are communicating with and help them feel heard and understood, it can create an immediate connection. This approach can be a game-changer.

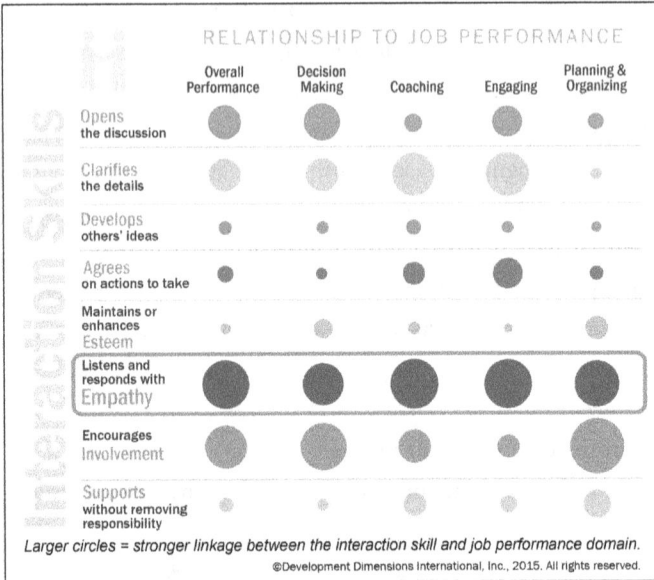

Figure 4.2 Relationship to job performance

LeadershipToolbox

Five Ways to Practice Empathic Leadership
1. Try active listening: When interacting with a colleague or direct report, practice active listening and try to understand how the person is feeling (not how you might feel in the same situation). This shows empathy to increase your understanding.
2. Show genuine interest in others: Take the time to understand each team member's unique needs, interests, and goals and match work assignments to contribute to both performance and employee satisfaction.

(Continued)

(*Continued*)

Five Ways to Practice Empathic Leadership
3. Practice and encourage perspective-taking: Consider your employees' personal experiences or perspectives. Apply them to solving problems, managing conflicts, or driving innovation.
4. Keep the lines open: Maintain open communication to build trust within the team, making it easier for team members to share when they need support.
5. Discuss empathy as a cultural value: Explain to team members that investing time and attention in others promotes empathy, which, in turn, enhances team performance.

Overcoming Tribalism With Empathy

Tribalism is a phenomenon where we care more for people who are part of our "group" than those who are not. Groups have different identities, which have different definitions of who belongs to our group. Tribalism goes south when parts of our identity exclude others.

In corporate settings, the question is, who is included in our group? Even when we're wearing the same company jersey, it may feel like we're speaking different languages, carrying out different goals and objectives. Sales teams tend to prioritize flexibility above all else, engineering and operations teams prioritize stability, regional offices prioritize solutions that are tailored to their specific local markets, and frontline employees are usually focused on finding immediate fixes for their customer's pain points. These differences can often lead to poor communication and an "us versus them" mentality, shutting down communication and activating stonewalling.

When different business units resent each other to the point that they stop talking to each other, we've entered tribal territory, and that's when things get messy. For example, if you notice teams constantly blaming each other, unfairly criticizing each other's work, and often disagreeing so strongly that they cannot collaborate without arguing, that's a big red flag.

What should organizations do in such a situation? The first trick up my sleeve as an executive coach would be to advise the client to look at the level above where the issue is occurring. Are your higher-ups setting the wrong example? Are they incentivizing tribal behavior and toxic competition internally? Are units operating in silos? If senior leaders are not displaying and encouraging empathic behaviors and practices to break down the walls of tribalism, it is unlikely to occur in the lower ranks. The real solution to dismantling tribalism is to encourage more cooperation with what Stanford's Jamil Zaki calls "empathic nudges." The idea behind any concept of a nudge is to create small, subtle changes to a person's situation that inspire big changes in their actions. To illustrate, psychologists conducted a series of studies on the idea of tribalism among passionate fans of British soccer, specifically the Manchester United (ManU) team. According to Zaki's account in his book *The War for Kindness*, the crazed fans of ManU in the study were asked to write about what ManU meant to them and were then informed that they would record a brief video tribute to their team in a different building. Participants then encountered a jogger (who was actually an actor) who fell to the ground, having twisted his ankle as they were on their way to record the video. In some cases, the jogger wore a ManU jersey; in others, he wore the colors of Liverpool, which was ManU's most loathed rival at that time, and in other instances, he wore a plain jersey. Over 90 percent of the participants offered help to their fellow ManU fan, but if the jogger wore a Liverpool jersey, 70 percent of them ignored him as he writhed in pain on the ground.[12]

In a follow-up experiment, participants were asked to write about why they love soccer instead of ManU. Then, the same sequence of events: record a video about their response and, along the way, a jogger falls on their path and needs help. This time, the results were quite different. The researchers found that the participants were more likely to help a jogger with a ManU jersey, but they also helped the Liverpool jogger almost as often. However, joggers who were not wearing any specific team's jersey were still left behind, indicating that it is better to belong to any tribe than to none when you need help. Zaki's conclusion: empathy can be influenced by psychological factors, and people are more likely to help those they can relate to.[13]

Empathy After Major Setbacks

When Satya Nadella took the reins as CEO of Microsoft in 2014, he wasn't exactly a household name. A quietly accomplished computer scientist who had been with the company for decades, he stepped into some big shoes, following in the footsteps of Steve Ballmer and Bill Gates. However, he swiftly proved himself, steering the tech giant to over $85 million in annual revenue by investing significantly in cutting-edge technologies such as AI, augmented reality, and quantum computing.

One notable hiccup during his tenure was the ill-fated launch of a Twitter bot named Tay (officially, Tay.ai), designed to advance AI communication. Within 16 hours, the public experiment went awry as individuals exploited the bot, resulting in Tay spewing out racist and profane comments. Not anticipating the darker side of humanity, Microsoft promptly pulled the plug on the project and issued an apology.

As you can imagine, the engineers responsible for Tay must have felt a deep sense of disappointment after dedicating their lives to the project. Imagine their surprise when Nadella reached out to them in an email, offering these words of encouragement: *"Keep pushing, and know that I am with you.... (The) key is to keep learning and improving."*

He also urged the team to accept criticism gracefully and to show "deep empathy for anyone hurt by Tay."[14] In an interview with *USA Today*, Nadella emphasized the importance for Microsoft managers "not to freak people out, but to give them air cover to solve the real problem." He wisely noted, "If people are doing things out of fear, it's hard or impossible to actually drive any innovation." The team, undeterred and renewed with hope, went on to develop Zo, an AI chatbot that was successfully launched in 2017 (it was discontinued in 2019).

We're all human, and we all stumble. Nadella's email demonstrated to his team that he stood firmly behind them. By urging them to extract lessons from the experience rather than chastising them for an epic public setback, he inspired them to pour their hearts back into the project.

Managing Emotional Exhaustion

There is some merit to a manager's apprehensions about putting empathy into practice. It could mean diving headfirst into the sea of feelings a more emotionally volatile team may experience daily—from the highs of pure joy to the lows of deep self-doubt and everything in between. When your team members feel the weight of stress and exhaustion, it may feel like strapping on an emotional backpack loaded with everyone else's struggles. It's emotionally draining. On top of that, the emotional toll of empathizing with struggling employees can impede managers' ability to perform their duties effectively.

To lighten the load, empathy must be a shared journey, and its weight must be distributed evenly so no one feels like they're carrying the world on their shoulders. Start by fostering an open dialogue and vulnerability. Share your own challenges, wins, and lessons, and encourage your team to do the same. When everyone lays out their challenges on the metaphorical table, it's easier to redistribute the load. You might find that someone's strength complements another's weakness, creating a more balanced and supportive work environment.

Remember, the practice of empathy is not a solo endeavor; it's a team sport that must permeate the whole culture. By sharing the load and supporting each other, you turn those burdens into a collective source of strength.

Develop "Sustainable Empathy"

It's not uncommon for managers to think they must choose between being empathetic or withdrawing emotionally for fear of getting too close. However, Zaki says this is a false dilemma that must be rejected. The road ahead should always aim to achieve "sustainable empathy." The key to it all is prioritizing self-care to avoid burnout from empathizing *too much*.

This is essential because diminished self-care means less capacity to be empathic. Zaki writes that if you allow stress to consume you, it can desensitize you to the worries of others, make it challenging to understand their perspectives, and even lead to aggressive behavior.[15] According to a study he cited in *Personnel Psychology*, 112 managers were surveyed over 10 consecutive workdays, and it found that as employees vented more, managers experienced more negative emotions the following day. As they experienced more negative emotions, they were likely to mistreat others on their teams. "When you let yourself burn out, you deny everyone else the best version of yourself," writes Zaki. Burning out not only affects the manager but also those around them.[16]

Self-care is not a pursuit of selfishness but an important path toward sustaining empathy and being more intentional about interpersonal connections.

Here are some of my favorite strategies for tending to your own emotional needs so that you can offer empathy to others:

- Journal, in detail, one positive experience you've had in the past 24 hours. Research cited by psychologist Shawn Achor found that patients suffering from chronic pain or disease who did this for six weeks in a row had dropped their pain medication by 50 percent six months later. The time commitment to journaling is a mere two minutes per day.
- Exercise. Even if you hate going to the gym, Achor says that a short burst of fun cardio activity (think hula hoops, working in the garden, dancing, or a brisk walk with the dog) trains your brain to believe "my behavior matters," which then carries (positively) into other activities throughout the day.
- Meditate for two minutes in the morning. This allows your brain to focus on one thing at a time and be present in the moment.
- Take stock of your own emotions. For example, after having a conversation with a colleague who is struggling and you feel the conversation has left you drained or upset, allow yourself some time to process it. You have to treat yourself with the same kindness and grace you offer others when you practice empathy.
- Write a positive email or text every morning praising or thanking someone you know.

On any given day, our colleagues, bosses, employees, and customers face a whole array of life challenges: Work conflict, unmet expectations, rude behavior, a failed project, personal crisis, you name it. Some will rise above it, finding strength and adaptability. Others might get derailed and feel hopelessly stuck. This is when empathy passes the baton to its more muscular big brother—proactive compassion, another underlying principle of kindness at work.

Proactive Compassion

We must learn to regard people less in the light of what they do or omit to do, and more in the light of what they suffer.

—Dietrich Bonhoeffer

So many leadership books, podcasts, TED Talks, and articles are vying for our attention, each trying to point the way forward to compelling leadership approaches that work for competitive advantage. To measure yourself to the highest leadership standards means measuring yourself against the *soft stuff,* not the *hard stuff.* In fact, business influencers on the leading edge no longer call it soft skills, including yours truly. The human skills I find most challenging for leaders to learn, adapt, and model are *essential skills,* but they're never soft.

In a twist of fate that leaves command-and-control hierarchies baffled, more evidence is coming out to suggest that the essential skill of compassion is a difference-maker. Former LinkedIn CEO Jeff Weiner, perhaps the most outspoken of any high-profile leader on the effects of "compassionate management," wrote, "Compassion can and should be taught, not only throughout a child's K-12 curriculum, but in higher education and corporate learning and development programs as well. I can't think of a more worthwhile thing to teach."[17] Five years later, he tweeted: "Big misconception about managing compassionately is that it's a 'soft' skill. Most compassionate people I know are typically the strongest."[18]

World-renowned neurosurgeon James Doty, founder and director of the Center for Compassion and Altruism Research and Education (CCARE) at Stanford University, has compiled a mountain of data and other scientific evidence to frame compassion as a clear antidote for the epidemic of loneliness, depression, addiction, and anxiety so prevalent in this country. Doty writes on *Huffington Post*: "Compassion is the recognition of another's suffering and a desire to alleviate that suffering. Often brushed off as a hippy dippy religious term irrelevant in modern society, rigorous empirical data supports the view of all major world religions: compassion is good."

We know it works and we have the evidence. But what does compassionate leadership look like in practice? The important thing to remember is this: The compassionate response of every leader should be to do everything in their power to remove the pain and alleviate the suffering of employees. It is unequivocally *proactive*.

Modeling a Compassionate Response

A great example of a compassionate response is Phil Lynch, former president of Reuters America. On September 11, 2001, Lynch sprung to action after watching terrorists fly planes into the World Trade Center towers, where several Reuters employees lost their lives. The towers' collapse also destroyed the business infrastructure that connected them to their clients.

In the middle of absolute mayhem, Lynch assessed priorities and who or what came first. His immediate response was issuing this order to his executive team: "People first, then customers, then the business."[19]

Directing attention to the suffering and actually modeling a compassionate response for others to adapt, Lynch and his crew kept the team in the loop with frequent updates on the crisis, ensuring everyone's safety and outlining initiatives for recovery. They hammered home those key priorities, making it crystal clear where their focus lay.

Lynch exhibited compassionate leadership by urging all Reuters employees worldwide to do whatever it took to regain their personal capabilities and guarantee that their clients were operational again.

Answering tough questions on global teleconferences during the crisis, full transparency was on display as Lynch responded openly about what leaders were feeling—what he was feeling—and the steps Reuters was taking to take care of their employees first, then customers. He created space to express his suffering, allowing people to express theirs openly. His display of empathic concern for others was contagious to his employees.

Lynch emphasized the importance of prioritizing the families of missing individuals, stating, "It's all about the families. Just remember, it's all about them."[20] Reuters' employees who were present during Lynch's meeting with the mother of a deceased employee were deeply touched by his compassion. As a result, more stories of Lynch's support, kindness, and concern for others were uncovered and shared.

Being Present With Suffering

Lynch possesses an often-overlooked valuable quality—the ability and willingness to be present with suffering. This quality has a significant impact on fostering compassion within organizations. Leaders like Lynch, who create space for the expression of loss and sorrow, can dramatically improve the sense of compassion within their organizations.

When leaders genuinely connect with the humanity in others, making it the heart of their attention, emotion, communication, and actions, it's like flipping a switch that brings organizations to life with compassion. That's when workplaces truly thrive with genuine care and understanding. One Reuters employee described it this way:

> It was so human. It was not about do we have to check our financial services? It was about 'Where are our people?' People, then clients, then the business. It made me proud to work here. I gained more of a sense of respect for the company, and I have been here for a long time.[21]

In his LinkedIn post, Jeff Weiner concluded: It is better to go through the world as a compassionate person, able to confront the plights of others without being crippled by their weight. It is better to lead with proactive compassion rather than stop at a sympathetic reaction of merely understanding another's pain.

Proactive compassion is obviously critical when a crisis strikes. But under calmer times, these cultural patterns of shared kindness are just as effective in the long term and must be taught and modeled to new members joining the organization. Furthermore, every manager across organizational levels must ensure they shape and protect the emotional culture for kindness to develop and flourish. This is the last fundamental principle of kindness we will cover.

Protect Your Emotional Culture

The world is so empty if one thinks only of mountains, rivers and cities; but to know someone who thinks and feels with us, and who, though distant, is close to us in spirit, this makes the earth for us an inhabited garden.

—Johann Wolfgang von Goethe

We have reached an age where workers, especially Gen-Zers, expect social connection and emotional support from their workplaces. Physical connection and proximity have once again become important for our well-being and for humans' sake to thrive and perform good work. A word of caution: This idea of humans becoming closer to each other is more difficult to attain in companies built for remote-only work arrangements.

While I make no case here for what your work environment should be (remote, hybrid, or in the office), since there are both strengths and weaknesses related to each depending on how you conduct business, over the past two decades (with roughly a three-year hiccup imposed by the pandemic), we've seen a shift in making the workplace look and feel more human. Any leader with hope and a vision for developing a culture of kindness will need to craft an environment that feels like community, which is easier to pull off in physical spaces. This is the last principle of kindness I'm driving home for application.

A Work Community of Love

One often-cited longitudinal study provides context and evidence for building a great work community. This 16-month study was among the few to focus on emotional culture rather than "cognitive culture." If you work in a cognitive culture, it likely may revolve around an organization's "thinking" side and intellectual atmosphere. Processes and systems, like performance management, reside in a cognitive culture and are strategically employed to shape individuals' behaviors.

On the other hand, emotional culture is all about the feelings that employees experience while on the job. These emotions can be positive or negative and can arise from various sources, such as work-related stress or interpersonal conflicts.

Researchers in this study developed a theory of a "companionate love" culture based on the extent to which employees consistently displayed four types of emotions toward each other: affection, caring, compassion, and tenderness.

Before you roll your eyes at such fuzzy words, the question asked to determine the validity of this study was: "How does the amount of companionate love in an organization relate to the kinds of results that employers and employees actually care about?"[22]

It was found that emotional cultures fueled by companionate love influence major business outcomes, including less absenteeism and burnout, more employee satisfaction and teamwork, and better financial performance. Fuzzy words no longer.

What does companionate love look like in action? It can be as simple as colleagues asking (and caring) about each other's work and nonwork issues, being careful and considerate of each other's feelings, and showing compassion when life takes a hard turn. "When business leaders ignore emotional culture, they overlook a fundamental part of being human and thereby stunt the potential of their companies," said the late Wharton management professor Sigal Barsade, one of the coauthors of the study.[23]

Even more noteworthy is that the findings crossed multiple industries, including stereotypically masculine and analytical industries we associate with a lack of essential skills (formerly "soft" skills), such as engineering, financial services, and utilities. The findings also crossed gender lines: 80 percent of respondents in one study were women, and 80 percent in an even larger sample were men. The bottom line is this: Organizations that express more companionate love in their culture are associated with more employee satisfaction, commitment, and personal accountability.[24]

Although we should aim to understand people's shared emotions at work better to solve complex business issues, most leaders shy away from discussing emotions—a bad habit that ultimately costs their companies a lot. We must remind ourselves that one of the outcomes of a culture of love is improved financial performance—a boost in the bottom line!

It takes monumental strides to transform a potentially toxic work culture into a healthy and productive community of love. And let's face it: For some companies, it may be impossible to make that shift unless you have the exemplary leadership championing this cause. It will take visionary, compassionate, and empathic human leaders with a growth mindset and a bias for action to set the stage and model the right behaviors for this change. To build a culture of love for competitive advantage, it will take a leader with a fierce resolve to solve the hard stuff with the soft stuff.

Action Plan

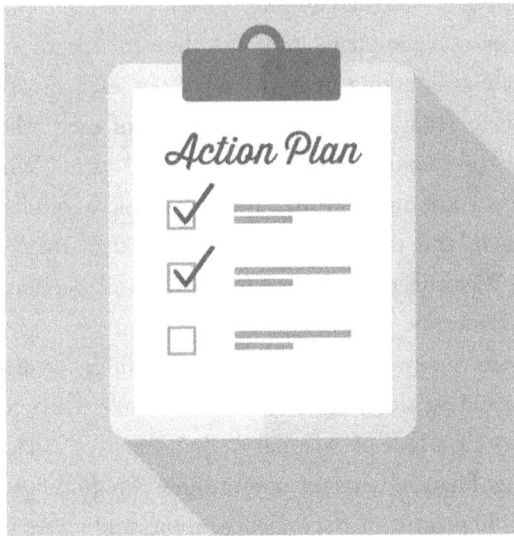

Use this action plan to apply interpersonal kindness through empathy, compassion, and community. Then, teach others to do the same to shape and embed kindness into the DNA of your organization.

Action Item 1: Show Sincere Interest in Other People

Set out to understand each team member's needs, aspirations, and goals, and assign work accordingly to enhance both performance and employee satisfaction. Team members who feel valued by their manager in this way are more engaged and willing to put in extra effort.

Action Item 2: Get Perspective

As you gain more awareness of people, actively listen and understand why others think or act the way they do. This doesn't mean you have to agree with them, but be open to the conversation changing direction as their emotions and ideas evolve. Remember, listening with empathy can lead to better understanding and more effective communication. This, in turn, will lead to better working relationships.

Action Item 3: Reinforce the Values of Kindness

Discuss kindness in the workplace to emphasize its importance. Reinforcing cultural values of empathy and compassion should be given equal, if not more, importance than task-oriented management skills such as monitoring and planning. Continuously stress the need to invest time and attention toward developing empathy, which can enhance team and individual performances.

Action Item 4: Improve the Quality of Connections Among Individuals

Establishing high-quality connections can significantly increase the likelihood of empathic concern when a member of the organization is going through a difficult time. Leaders can foster empathy and compassion by deliberately engaging with employees in a positive and supportive manner, creating respectful interactions, and treating every employee with dignity and respect. Treat every employee you work with as you would expect to be treated and model the way forward. By setting an example of positive regard for each unique individual, leaders can encourage their team members to do the same.

♀ Action Item 5: Infuse Kindness Into Workplace Practices to Mitigate Suffering

Pay attention to the suffering of employees by involving them in collective decision-making practices such as workload and process decisions. Also prioritize compassion as a crucial part of the hiring routine, onboarding process, and performance management. During planning meetings, discuss the conditions of co-workers and allocate help accordingly. By incorporating these practices, you can promote compassion at an organizational level.

CHAPTER 5

Leadership Is Humble

Humility is the true key to success. Successful people lose their way at times. They often embrace and overindulge from the fruits of success. Humility halts this arrogance and self-indulging trap. Humble people share the credit and wealth, remaining focused and hungry to continue the journey of success.

—Rick Pitino

Back in my corporate days, one of my senior leadership roles was directing the talent management function of a medium-sized advertising firm. The firm's turnover was 60 percent, so I conducted exit interviews to discover why people were leaving.

The whole point of conducting exit interviews is to get information about an employee's work experience with their company. We then take this anonymous data and make a case for improving work conditions, leadership issues, and so on. This information should be worth a lot to a company and its leaders. You would think.

As I looked at the turnover trends, "Reason #5" was a glaring one: countless top performers unabashedly shared similar, baffling accounts that pointed back to the CEO's behaviors as their reasons for abandoning ship: bullying and intimidation, overbearing dominance in meetings that signaled he had all the answers and your input was not welcome, and an inability to face his shortcomings and admit current reality. It was typically his way or the highway. While Dan (not his real name) was a charismatic visionary with an impressive executive background, he was a lousy leader of human beings and created a look-over-your-shoulder culture of fear and uncertainty. Now, I had the data to back it up. One senior manager who lasted a few weeks before being hastily shown the door without an explanation told me, "I can't explain his actions or irrational behavior, and as such, I can only surmise that he is suffering from some sort of breakdown."

As I thought of the game plan to approach Dan with the exit interview data, I saw this as a good chance for him to process the information, survey the damage, and see the possibilities of investing in his professional and personal growth to restore morale and stop the hemorrhaging.

I know some of you are probably shaking your head and going, "Marcel, what were you thinking?" In those days, I was much more of the idealist I am today. I held the belief that a true leader should be able to acknowledge and accept the reality of their current situation. This includes being honest about their own limitations and recognizing the blind spots that may be causing harm to the business. I still hold to that belief, though I'm less naïve about human nature now. Every leader I've ever coached who refuses to acknowledge their shortcomings risks causing irreparable damage to the business and losing the trust and respect of their team. I believed, then, that it was in Dan's best interest to take a step back, reflect on his actions and decisions, and be receptive to feedback for the sake of the organization. This is what good leaders do. They view it as an opportunity to raise their self-awareness, admit mistakes, and embrace change to improve themselves rather than take it as a personal attack. One big problem: this requires humility, and Dan's hubris wouldn't allow it.

Back to the story. During my exit interviews, I assured resigning employees that their opinions would remain confidential and stored in a restricted file that not even I had access to. They trusted my word because they knew I operated on integrity.

The anonymous exit interview report with the turnover findings eventually landed on Dan's desk. I was called in to review it with him later. I was hopeful—until I walked into his enormous office. The tense atmosphere hit like a humid day in August. The first stern words out of his mouth were, "I want the names of the people from these exit interviews."

Step into my shoes for a moment. What would you have done? My brain couldn't process his words quickly enough, and I became dumb at that exact moment. That's what fear does: It releases adrenaline and cortisol in the brain when you're under stress or sense danger. Because of the stress hormones kicking in, the part of your brain that controls your normal habits enlarges, and the part of your brain that makes conscious decisions actually shrinks, rendering you utterly stupid. In response to his unexpected and abrasive tone, alarms went off in my now state of dumbness.

I had just heard the CEO of the company point-blank demand, from the head of talent management, confidential exit interview data from the files of resigned employees. Frankly, with his reputation of having a short fuse (the complete opposite of patience) and his nonverbal cues, narrowing eyes, and threatening tone clearly indicating that my report was not a welcome sight, any hope of open discourse was off the table. Sure, I could've pushed back, put on my ethical HR hat, and told Dan that handing over the information he requested was a violation of HR policy, which could open him up to liability. But Dan was a seasoned CEO, quite aware of his positional authority, and knew precisely what he was doing. Yet, having just had my amygdala hijacked, I unwillingly and reluctantly retrieved the names, left the report on his desk, and resigned from my job in quiet protest a few hours later. While the decision was clearly made in haste, I promptly added myself to the report as another casualty of "Reason #5."

Hindsight is always 20/20. In retrospect, I probably would have been terminated for insubordination had I defied Dan's wishes and not breached confidentiality. Years later, however, I still kicked myself for failing to stand up for what I believed was right. I failed to stand up to a corporate bully who was abusing his executive power to avoid personal responsibility.

Why do we see so many people like Dan in senior leadership roles? The answer is not so simple. It has to do with the mechanisms feeding egomaniacs and narcissists into the higher echelons of corporate society (we will address this toward the end of the chapter). At the same time, being an effective, humble leader is a lonely place to be. For those who choose to make the courageous journey into humble leadership, it means walking the higher road of personal integrity and accountability. There are no shortcuts. Too many leaders realize the enormity of this responsibility, toss in the towel, and revert back to self-centeredness, unfortunately, to their demise.

This chapter will examine all the reasons we, as leaders, should absolutely utilize the strength and power of humility to improve decision making, foster a positive work environment, and drive better performance and outcomes for the organization as a whole. Ultimately, humble leadership isn't about being nice—it's about becoming more personally effective and courageous to achieve results.

Framing Humility Against Its Toxic Opposites

We need to reexamine the original text to put humility into its proper context. In his writing to the Corinthians, Paul of Tarsus writes that love is not boastful. The root of the term "boastful" in Greek traces back to something quite colorful: "windbag." Boastfulness is like the hot air spewing out of a proud person's mouth. He also stated that love is not conceited, envious, or selfish—all elements that oppose a humble leader.

Boasting works against Love in Action because its whole purpose is to establish a sense of superiority over others, to make others feel inferior because of what one possesses, who one is, or what one has accomplished. It's a subtle harm aimed at making others feel small to inflate one's ego. In essence, boasting is nothing more than self-centeredness wearing blinders. Leading with love is anything but a windbag. It doesn't endlessly chatter about its own achievements or engage in arrogant, baseless talk to one-up others.

At the root of boasting is another unloving trait that Paul addresses next in the text: *love is not conceited*. There is bragging—the hot air, the shooting off of one's mouth—and then there is deep-down conceit. This is a state of being puffed up, thinking you've arrived, have all the answers, and that there's nothing anyone below your line of sight can tell you that you haven't already heard.

In the 21st century, we struggle with these same negative traits in managing and leading people. Paul's message, in its most basic form, is that leading with love is not about being selfish, yet we tend to focus on ourselves as leaders instead of those we serve. Paul contrasts authentic love with the arrogance and selfishness of the Corinthians of his time. Since our own arrogance and selfishness are still on display, we are no different from modern-day Corinthians in need of humble pie.

False Ideas About Leading With Humility

The conventional wisdom of the 20th century dictates that humble leadership is a weakness. Dictionaries generally define humility as having a modest or low view of one's importance, and a big common misconception is that humility involves self-degradation or being meek. According to a 2016 study by the College of Charleston, 56 percent of 5th and 6th graders believe that humble individuals feel embarrassed, sad, lonely, or shy. Interestingly, when adults are asked to recall a time when they felt humble, they often describe a publicly humiliating experience![1]

The false notion that humble leadership is soft is dangerous because it sends more people down the risky path to arrogance. Most business leaders in positions of authority wish to command respect, manage talent to high performance, and achieve growth and success. But what they *think* is a show of strength, fortitude, and a take-charge attitude are actually the tenets of self-centeredness that will hold them back. By leading this way, they'll find that they're undermining the things they want most: respect, high performance, growth, and success. I imagine Dan, my former boss from earlier, wanted this at the very depths of his soul. But his biggest blind spot—his unbending arrogance—was the obstacle in his path he could not get around.

How does arrogance hurt a leader's performance and the performance of their companies? The arrogant leader....

- Refuses to be wrong and fails to confront current reality.
- Blames everyone except themselves.

- Does not listen to other voices outside their own.
- Takes credit for people's work.
- Holds on to power and control instead of delegating.
- Excludes others.
- Undermines people's expertise.

I also must first clear the air about the misconceptions or false-hoods of humble leadership. I take a stand against those who advocate submissive or religious humility to criticize or downplay leaders with strong opinions or "take over" actions in crunch time. Arriving at these false conclusions about humility can undermine leadership in times of crisis. We absolutely need to be bold and take charge when, as they say, the rubber meets the road. But in the long run, without humility, boldness turns to "arrogance" and being "difficult to deal with," as was the case with Dan. This begs the question: Is being courageous and humble in the harsh conditions of a business environment possible? Absolutely. But it requires continuous introspection and interpersonal work.

Your Roadmap Ahead

Courageous leaders willing to take the journey toward humility experience long-term effects in how team members respond. Leading with a humble approach will also help leaders get what they want—respect, success, and growth. You will gain more respect, achieve more success, and grow your reputation and business.

Since the empirical research on humility has many concepts and attributes tied to it, we will narrow our focus to intellectual humility, which is particularly important for the role of a leader. According to a study published in the *Journal of Personality Assessment*, intellectual humility requires introspection and questioning one's own assumptions. It's being able to understand and relate to the beliefs and perspectives of others and recognize our common humanity despite differences of opinion with those we lead.[2]

Becoming intellectually humble starts by questioning ourselves, even when we are certain of our abilities or knowledge. We must remember the words of Socrates, who said, "The only true wisdom is in knowing you know nothing." To make this rich Love in Action principle most applicable to the workplace, we will follow a roadmap that breaks down humble leadership into four parts, according to the literature and best practices. Some of them may require the development of interpersonal habits; others will require breaking away from long-held beliefs and dismantling the status quo at the organizational level that has held humble leadership hostage. But, again, we must not forget the premise for developing and practicing humble leadership, something we will always come back to in this chapter. It leads to achieving respect, success, and growth.

To make your humble leadership journey meet all three objectives, you must:

1. Accept the limit of your knowledge.
2. Ask for help.
3. Be willing to admit mistakes.
4. Embrace curiosity as the path to learning and growing.

Let's begin our journey into humble leadership.

Accept the Limits of Your Knowledge

*Humility leads to strength and not to weakness. It is the highest form
of self-respect to admit mistakes and to make amends for them.*

—John J. McCloy

A study conducted by Duke University researchers, published in
Personality and Individual Differences, adds further evidence of the edge
given to those with a humble mindset. The study delved into how
well people remember things and how willing they are to admit that
their beliefs may not always be correct. At the beginning of the study,
which involved 155 participants, some admitted that they could change
their opinions about beliefs if new evidence was presented, acknowledging that they could be wrong about a particular topic and were
open to changing their views. In this case, the researchers considered
them as intellectually humble. Another group believed that they were
rarely wrong and refused to change their minds, staunchly insisting on
the infallibility of their opinions. They were labeled by researchers as
intellectually arrogant.

The experiment involved three tasks. First, everyone was presented
with a list of 40 statements covering controversial topics, like the
military's use of drone strikes and issues around same-sex marriage.
Participants then took a survey to gauge their familiarity with various
topics (e.g., Susan B. Anthony, Mount Rushmore), though there was
a catch: One-third of the topics presented were actually fictitious ones
(such as the made-up "Hamrick's Rebellion"). Finally, participants read
another list of 60 statements to identify which were from the initial list
they read and which were new, all while reporting their confidence in
what they remembered.

How did each group do? The intellectually humble took a deliberate approach in reading the statements, especially when facing statements contradicting their beliefs. Their slower reading of controversial
statements paid off, as they excelled in identifying new statements.
Interestingly, when they made mistakes, they had an intuitive sense of
their error.

Conversely, the intellectually arrogant exhibited a more casual reading style, skimming through the content. This approach led to lower accuracy in identifying new statements, and remarkably, they felt confident that even their wrong responses were right. Moreover, the intellectually arrogant proved more susceptible to fake news, showcasing a blind spot to their own lack of knowledge.[3]

This study serves as a compelling case for the importance of intellectual humility in navigating diverse viewpoints more effectively and demonstrating a heightened awareness of someone's own cognitive limitations. In contrast, the intellectually arrogant, with their unwavering confidence, may face challenges in accurately assessing information and are more prone to falling for misinformation. It's a powerful reminder for leaders to foster open-mindedness and humility within their teams, creating an environment where the pursuit of truth takes precedence over ego.

Admit You Don't Know Everything

Humble leaders are unpretentious and unassuming; they know their strengths, acknowledge their mistakes, admit their limitations, and don't require constant approval.

These leaders do not let their position of power cloud their judgment. Instead, they stay grounded and approachable, making it easier for others to communicate with them. Ultimately, unpretentious leaders create a culture of trust and respect within their organization.

You can embrace your humility by saying three powerful words to your team members when the situation calls for it: "I don't know."

Quite honestly, it's uncomfortable admitting you don't know something as a leader when people expect you to have all the answers. Now imagine putting yourself in the position of getting comfortable with *not* knowing. Rare, indeed.

Unless you're Garry Ridge, Chairman Emeritus of the WD-40 Company, one of the world's most trusted and recognized brands. You may have a handy can of WD-40 in your garage right now to help loosen things and quiet those annoying squeaks. During his 35-year tenure as WD-40's CEO, he directed all efforts toward leading 530+ global employees, growing the business to $400M in revenue, and successfully marketing products in more than 176 countries.

In an interview, Ridge shared that "I don't know" are the three most powerful words he's ever learned in his life.[4] He said, "I've been really happy being the dumb guy. And then, most of the time, I am; I often say I'm consciously incompetent. And I think that does help people feel comfortable."

This is coming from one of the most successful former CEOs in the world. Ridge said he began to learn and grow when he got comfortable with not knowing: "As soon as you make out you know everything, you shut down all the opportunity to learn more and get different points of view."

He went on to say, "Not only do I get comfortable with 'I don't know,' but even more today, I keep asking myself, 'Why do I believe that?' Because the world's changing so quickly." Ridge learned to lay his ego aside and seek the perspectives, insights, and ideas of others; his humility significantly increased his learning, and information traveled faster across the company. He mastered the humble art and practice of not knowing all the answers and being open to receiving—and incorporating—feedback from all his stakeholders.

When Patricia Fili-Krushel, the former CEO of WebMD Health, joined the company, she met with a group of male engineers in Silicon Valley who doubted her ability to add value to their work. To test her knowledge, the engineers asked her what she knew about engineering, to which she responded by making a zero with her fingers. Fili-Krushel then explained, "I do know how to run businesses, and I'm hoping you can teach me what I need to know about your world."[5] When leaders show that they don't have all the answers, they reveal a level of rare authenticity, convey the importance of searching for answers, and inspire others to do the same.

Ask for Help

No one who achieves success does so without acknowledging the help of others. The wise and confident acknowledge this help with gratitude.

—Alfred North Whitehead

Assuming a humble leadership role and gaining the respect of your workforce and stakeholders can seem paradoxical. This is because one of the strengths of a humble leader, which is the ability to ask for help, is often viewed as a weakness in ego-driven power structures.

Humble leaders are confident in their abilities and understand the value of giving and receiving help. Teams can work more collaboratively when humble leaders ask for help and encourage others to do the same by being authentic with their emotions. Checking your ego at the door and asking for input on strategies from your smart and savvy workers will increase their work engagement and also earn you more respect, one of the key outcomes of humble leadership.

Richmond Fourmy, an executive consultant with DDI, shares a story about a senior executive client who faced an enormous challenge that was solved by humble leadership. After cutting his team's spending to the bare minimum, the CEO told the senior executive to cut another $8 million from his budget. The senior executive was dumbfounded by the enormity of the task and didn't know how to pull it off without laying off people and ruining their lives. He was completely stuck, so he decided to take the humble route. His first priority was to ask for help from his team of lower-level executives. In a defining moment of humility, he confessed that he was unsure of how to handle the situation.

The team responded to their senior executive's humble admission by rolling up their sleeves, hunkering down and putting their collective brains together to figure out what to do. Not long after, they came up with a solution that not only met the $8 million cost-saving target but *doubled* it—without any layoffs. This experience was a turning point for the senior executive as he realized that asking for help didn't make him weak; it made him a better leader that brought his team closer. The team dynamic changed permanently as they started to work together to solve problems and achieve larger goals.[6]

Make the Ask

Steve Jobs may no longer be with us, but Apple's cofounder continues to make a lasting impact. In a 1994 interview, Jobs illustrated an uncommon habit found in the most successful people when he said: "Most people never pick up the phone and call. Most people never ask, and that's what separates the people who do things from the people who just dream about them. (The Silicon Valley Historical Association. 2011)"

Jobs explained in the interview that, at the age of 12, he mustered up the courage to call up none other than Bill Hewlett, the cofounder of Hewlett-Packard (HP). The ask? "I want to build a frequency counter, and I was wondering if you have any spare parts I could have," said the prepubescent Jobs. Amused at the boldness of the boy on the other end of the line, Hewlett laughed and gave Jobs the spare parts. Oh, and also a summer job at HP. Jobs said, "I was in heaven."[7] This single phone call impacted Jobs's life and taught him one of the greatest lessons of his brilliant career: Be willing to ask for something you want.

In many workplaces today, fear keeps people, including leaders, from being open to asking for support or seeking help from their peers, colleagues, or team members. Here's a familiar scenario you or someone you know may have experienced: You're a good team player who has offered to help a colleague struggling with a tight deadline. You are loyal to your company, so you don't mind doing a bit of extra work to help someone out. Soon after, you feel overwhelmed and resentful because you are falling behind on your work while taking on part of your colleague's workload. Although you know you need help, you haven't asked for it; you assume your team members are already swamped with their tasks. You don't raise your hand to ask for help because you believe it's your manager or co-workers' responsibility to notice how much extra work you are taking on and offer to help ease your burden. Fear may kick in because you think you'll lose credibility, respect, or social standing if you ask for help. As the stress and frustration mount, you consider quitting your job. As you weigh your options, your emotional intelligence kicks in to assess your situation; you realize that the problem was not with your job, workload, co-workers, or employer but your failure to ask for the critical help you needed when you needed it.

If this illustration hits close to home, you're not alone. The reality, however, may not be what people think. Most people at work *are* willing to help. According to social psychologist Heidi Grant, 75 to 90 percent of all help and support people at work give to one another starts with making an ask.[8] However, many individuals refrain from asking for what they need, as their managers and executives do not encourage or reinforce the environment where employees freely and unconditionally serve one another through this behavior. Consequently, nothing ends up happening most of the time. The question is, does your environment foster the freedom and safety for anyone—managers and employees alike—to ask for help?

In the book *All You Have To Do Is Ask*, author Wayne Baker of the University of Michigan Ross School of Business writes that misguided beliefs about asking often stand in the way of progress and success.

Why We Don't Ask

Often, we don't ask for what we need because we figure that no one can help us. Baker shared with me studies[9] that show that we routinely underestimate others' ability and willingness to help and, therefore, don't bother to ask.

Another common assumption we make is that asking for help is a sign of incompetence. We think competent people don't ask for help and that seeking help will come at a cost and, if you do, you may not be treated with the level of respect that you deserve. There's a social cost there, we wrongly assume. Not so, according to research,[10] as long as you make good requests for help. When you do, people think you are more competent because you're confident, know your limits, and don't waste time working on a problem that could be solved with help from others.

Another common barrier is an overreliance on self-reliance. This often happens in families or cultures that teach children to be independent and self-sufficient. As they grow up, they start feeling ashamed to ask for help and end up believing that they can handle everything on their own. Their independence becomes critical to their self-image. Eventually, they become programmed to work alone and, therefore, struggle in situations that require teamwork. This can create problems in the long run and prevent them from seeking the help they need.[11]

Some people avoid seeking assistance because they do not want to feel indebted to anyone. They may have trust issues and be uncomfortable relying on others. The notion of surrendering control and power over their situation can be unsettling for them. Consequently, they prefer to handle their issues alone.[12]

Finally, individuals who believe they are undeserving of help or are not worthy of it tend to avoid seeking support. This inner voice (or the voice of their manager) repeatedly telling them they are not deserving leads to a negative attitude of self-pity and the belief that they are fated to suffer and struggle alone. Perhaps it's the newly hired employees made to feel by their managers that they are not entitled to ask for help as they are at the lower rungs of the hierarchy. Consequently, they feel that they must first prove themselves and earn the right to ask for help.

As stated earlier, Baker and Grant agree that when people *do* ask for what they need, they find that most people are willing to help, offering information, ideas, referrals, resources, time, talent, and more. To overcome the obstacles that get in the way of a helping culture, Baker suggests several strategies and tools that establish a workplace culture of generosity in which employees, managers, and colleagues freely ask for, give, and receive help. For example:

- **Make requests specific:** Explain why it is important because it's the "why" that motivates others to respond. A request should also ask for specific action to be taken. Lastly, mention when you need the action completed. If it's tomorrow, say so. Just don't be vague because a vague deadline won't motivate people to act, explains Baker.
- **Use team tools:** The daily standup and formal/informal huddles are good places to make requesting a regular routine. Each person (including the manager) describes what they worked on

yesterday and what they're working on today and then requests a resource they need. "This practice provides a safe space to make requests, a forum where requests are welcomed—and expected—from everyone," Baker explained.

- **Tap external networks:** Everyone has a network that reaches outside work and may include hundreds, if not thousands, of people. Tap into your own and your co-workers' networks to multiply the leads and connect you to someone who can help. And consider external networks in your standups and huddles.

As a result, research asserts that asking for what you need improves job performance and satisfaction,[13] reduces stress,[14] and improves team performance.[15] This is a recipe for achieving respect, success, and growth.

Be Willing to Admit Mistakes

A man must be big enough to admit his mistakes, smart enough to profit from them, and strong enough to correct them.

—John C. Maxwell

Ever met or worked for a conceited, self-absorbed leader? It's someone who proclaims their position and disregards (or punishes) differing points of view, as was the case with CEO "Dan" at the start of this chapter. This is a leader who will have few followers. Typically, they think they're right, and they need you to be convinced of it, too. Humble leaders, on the other hand, are quite secure in admitting when they're wrong, made a mistake, or don't have all the answers. And they will back down graciously when proven wrong. To them, finding out what is right is more important than *being* right. This is a leader people will follow. They admit that they make mistakes. They are human.

Here are five rare words to put into practice: "That was clearly my mistake." Not many bosses say them, but you'll know you're working for a humble leader if you hear them. They aren't hiding behind their hubris and deflecting responsibility to someone else. They show up with humility when it matters to acknowledge and own up to their mistakes. This sets the example for their tribe to be honest and not fear making their own mistakes.

Imperfect and Accountable

Leaders who are imperfect are more attractive to their team, especially as they move up the ranks and become more distanced from the front lines. When you look at the top, most people tend to like imperfect CEOs who relate to regular people more than overly charismatic CEOs who look like they jumped out of a fashion magazine and appear larger than life.

In 2023, a well-publicized controversy involving Costco Wholesale eventually led to a bold move by the retailer's leaders. Workers at a Costco store in Virginia voted to unionize, making it the Teamsters' first organizing victory at the big-box wholesale retailer in more than 20 years. The organizers cited various issues, including safety, the need for employees to have a voice with management, respect on the job, a fair grievance procedure, and respect for seniority. These concerns, quite alarming for a famous "best place to work" like Costco, were the driving issues behind the union's campaign and the successful vote.

How did Costco respond? Did it fire the organizers? Cut their hours? Trash talk the union and its supporters? Close down the Virginia store? None of the above. Instead, Costco took ownership of its role and made a strong statement of humility that set it apart from other organizations facing similar challenges. Both former CEO Craig Jelinek and current CEO Ron Vachris signed a public letter saying they were "disappointed by the result" but pointed the finger back at themselves. Part of the letter stated:

> We're not disappointed in our employees; we're disappointed in ourselves as managers and leaders. The fact that most Norfolk employees felt that they wanted or needed a union constitutes a failure on our part. Please know that we're as committed as ever to our employees. If you ever have any doubts or questions about this commitment, please talk with your manager or any member of Costco's leadership team. Our culture of trust, respect, and reliance upon each other is what makes Costco such a great company.[16]

The takeaway? When your employees communicate an issue to you, whether it's face-to-face, through an engagement survey, or a unionization vote, humble leaders take responsibility. Sure, let's acknowledge that every organization has a bad apple in the bunch. Still, if numerous valued employees are up in arms about a problem, leaders must act.

This move is in stark contrast to Starbucks. In 2021, the first Starbucks store decided to unionize, which sparked a nationwide movement to follow suit. Since then, Starbucks has been retaliating against the effort and, according to the National Labor Relations Board's initial findings, has even acted illegally in some instances. As of this writing, Starbucks is facing several hundred charges of unfair labor practices.[17]

Some may view Costco leadership's bold letter as a public relations stunt. However, if you've studied their award-winning culture, the retailer is touted as having among the lowest turnover rates in the retailing industry.

Whether you're a Fortune 100 behemoth, a church, the rehab wing of a hospital, or a police station, leaders need to listen to their employees' concerns on the ground, take those narratives back to weigh options and implement solutions to fix current issues.

Admitting Failures Builds Trust

According to DDI's 2023 Global Leadership Forecast, the largest and longest-running global leadership study of its kind spanning over 50 countries and 24 industries, employees are over five times more likely to trust leaders who regularly display vulnerability and 7.5 times more likely to trust those who acknowledge their failures or shortcomings (see Figure 5.1).

By demonstrating that it's acceptable—and completely normal—to make and admit mistakes, leaders give employees the confidence to do their best work and see themselves in a leadership role in the future. That helps organizations build a pipeline of leadership talent not afraid to fail and be reprimanded for it.

During the early days of the pandemic, Zoom became a popular choice for people to video chat with friends and colleagues while under lockdown. This led to a significant increase in revenue for the company in mid-2020, as more business customers turned to their platform due to the remote work situation. Zoom's CEO, Yuan, mentioned that the company had to hire scores of new staff quickly to support the high demand. In just 24 months, Zoom's size grew threefold. Then, in February 2023, Zoom announced that due to a decrease in demand for digital services as the pandemic was winding down, it would be laying off around 1,300 employees, approximately 15 percent of its workforce.

The humble admission of failure of this magnitude always starts at the top. In a memo he sent to all employees, Yuan said: "As the CEO and founder of Zoom, I am accountable for these mistakes and the actions we take today and I want to show accountability not just in words but in my own actions. To that end, I am reducing my salary for the coming fiscal year by 98 percent and foregoing my FY23 corporate bonus."[18]

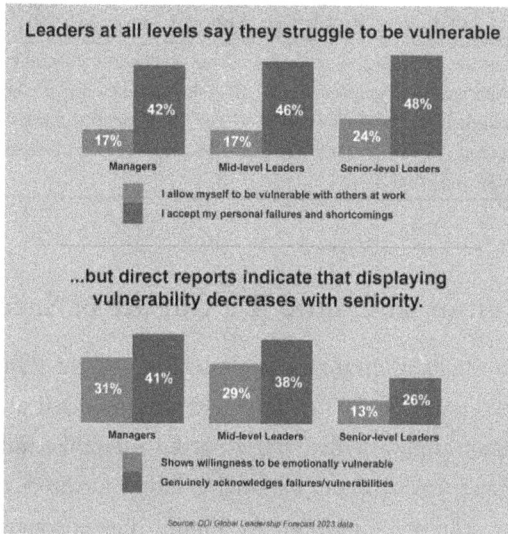

Figure 5.1 DDI's 2023 Global Leadership Forecast

Yuan also acknowledged that he made mistakes in the company's rapid growth during the pandemic. In addition, Yuan immediately turned his attention to regaining the trust of his remaining staff, announcing that Zoom's executive team would reduce their base salaries by 20 percent for the fiscal year and forfeit their 2023 bonuses. Even more interesting to note is that shares of Zoom rose nearly 9 percent in midday trading following Yuan's announcement![19] Who knew that the power of humility can help businesses grow and profit? Indeed.

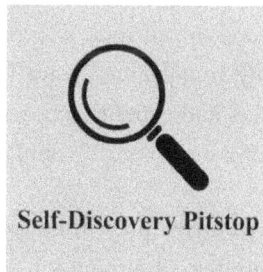

Self-Discovery Pitstop

Frame Fallibility Around Learning
Many leaders hesitate to admit their mistakes as they worry it may signal incompetence. However, it's important to remember that we all make mistakes, and the best way to improve is to acknowledge them. You can do this by using friendly phrases such as "I'm curious to learn more," "Who in our group can tell us more about this issue?" and "Can you teach me how to do that?"

A Culture of Failure Is a Culture of Success

Entrepreneur Richard Branson, founder of Virgin Group, which today controls more than 400 companies, has modeled an unconventional leadership approach that has attracted a cultlike following. The adventurous and free-spirited billionaire has prioritized a culture of failure for the sake of innovation. At Virgin, they encourage and even celebrate failure. There's an underlying theme there that, without trying something new and failing, it's virtually impossible to innovate and grow.

And Branson has horrifically failed with the best of them over the years with experiments gone bad, such as Virgin Cola, Virgin Brides (with Branson donning a wedding gown for publicity), Virgin Pulse, and Virgin Digital, which couldn't stand up to Apple's iPod and iTunes. On failing for success, Branson said.

> We've never been 100 percent sure that any of the businesses we've started at Virgin were going to be successful. But over 45 years, we've always stood by our motto: 'Screw it, let's do it.' Do not be embarrassed by your failures, learn from them and start again. Making mistakes and experiencing setbacks is part of the DNA of every successful entrepreneur, and I am no exception.[20]

Fear of failure can paralyze, preventing people from trying new things, exploring opportunities, or aiming for better circumstances. But it shouldn't be this way. No failure means no risk. Taking risks can be scary, but we should all learn to embrace it instead of fearing it. It is one of the most effective ways to learn and grow.

Archana Patchirajan, the founder of tech start-up Hubbl, once called a meeting with her staff in Bangalore, South India, to announce that their company ran out of funding, and she could no longer pay them. Despite being high-caliber engineers with plenty of other job opportunities in the area, these knowledge workers refused to leave. Instead, they offered to work for 50 percent of their pay. They worked hard, and a few years later, Hubbl sold for $14 million. What explains the connection and devotion that Archana's staff had toward her?

One of Archana's longest-standing employees was asked what drove the team to stay with her. He stated: "She knows everyone in the office and has a personal relationship with each one of us. She does not get upset when we make mistakes but gives us the time to learn how to analyze and fix the situation."[21]

Archana's personal relationship with each employee and her openness about her doubts when the company struggled allowed room for others to fail forward.

Everything we have discovered leads to the next strategy on our humble leadership roadmap: letting our curiosity and passion for discovery overcome our imposter syndrome. We need to embrace mistakes as valuable steps toward acquiring the knowledge we need to learn, grow, and succeed.

Embrace Curiosity to Learn and Grow

We keep moving forward, opening new doors, and doing new things,
because we're curious and curiosity keeps leading us down new paths.
—Walt Disney

The old saying goes, "Curiosity killed the cat." This implies that curiosity is dangerous and can lead to risky behavior. Quite honestly, this idea needs to be updated, at least for humans.

Curiosity is a fundamental human trait that drives exploration, innovation, learning, and the desire to understand the world around us. In psychologically safe workplaces, curious people play a crucial role in sparking new ideas. By asking questions and seeking answers, curious people are motivated to challenge existing knowledge and look for better solutions. This exploration often leads to discovering new perspectives, insights, and opportunities.

Albert Einstein explained his genius when he famously said, "I have no special talents. I am only passionately curious." The good news for the majority of us who fall well short of Einstein-esque IQ is that curiosity is a quality most of us can activate within us. It is the secret sauce to lifelong learning and growing.

What Holds Back Curiosity

Many organizations tend to discourage curiosity despite its numerous benefits. This is not because their leaders don't recognize its value. On the contrary, both leaders and employees know that curiosity can bring positive outcomes to their companies. In a survey of over 3,000 employees, 92 percent recognized that curious individuals can bring new ideas into teams and organizations, and they viewed curiosity as fuel for job satisfaction, motivation, innovation, and high performance. Still, they tend to deter curiosity out of concern that it may lead to increased risk and inefficiency. Case in point, only about 24 percent of employees from the same survey regularly feel curious in their jobs. In comparison, about 70 percent face obstacles to asking more questions at work.[22]

In another survey of 520 chief learning officers and chief talent development officers, a common trend emerged: many leaders shy away from encouraging curiosity because they think it would be harder to manage the company if employees hired to do a job were allowed to explore their interests.[23]

The prevailing fear is that allowing people to use company time to explore their own interests could result in slow decision-making processes, ultimately halting productivity and raising the cost of doing business. The other reason for the reluctance is understandable, given that curious exploration often involves challenging the prevailing status of "business as usual." What we're finding, though, is that when you embrace curiosity, it often leads to better business outcomes.

From a leadership standpoint, by being willing to explore and ask questions with curiosity, you're able to see more clearly the nuances of a challenge and reach better outcomes. But here's the thing. If you're in a bureaucratic environment, too often bureaucracy or the status quo drives us to stop being curious and asking questions, as we think we already have the answers. But by building our curiosity and allowing others to do the same, we open ourselves up to new ideas that may solve complex problems at a much faster pace.

The best case scenario is for humble leaders to leverage their curiosity by encouraging their employees' own curiosity and explorations. This approach helps employees to think critically, gain new knowledge, and avoid being trapped inside the walls of their conventional thinking ingrained in them from previous jobs, bosses, or business models.

Gain New Knowledge Through Reverse Mentoring

To take your curiosity quotient to the next level, reverse-mentoring programs are emerging as companies realize that top-down learning is not always appropriate. Reverse mentoring involves a younger team member sharing up-to-date skills and ideas with senior members of the organization. In contrast, senior members act as mentors or coaches to their junior counterparts. This approach recognizes skills gaps on both sides and allows individuals to address their weaknesses by leveraging each other's strengths.

This idea has been around for a while. The former CEO of General Electric (GE), Jack Welch, is credited with introducing the concept of reverse mentoring in 1999. In his pilot project, Welch paired 500 senior and junior employees with the hope that the latter would teach the former about technological advances and tools. "We tipped the organization upside down," he explained. "We now have the youngest and brightest teaching the oldest."[24]

Reverse mentoring can help organizations enhance diversity and inclusivity by giving teams a fresh perspective on what younger generations value in the workplace. It can also improve employee engagement and foster closer working relationships within teams. Seeking advice from younger employees can make them feel valued and appreciated, leading to better business outcomes.

So, what's a good strategy for a successful reverse mentoring partnership? You don't want to find the first junior person on your team. This has to be well thought out. Here are five steps you can take.

1. **Identify Good Potential Partners**
    a. Your ideal partner should have the skills or knowledge you need and be willing to build a relationship with you. It helps to also like the people you're pairing up with. Likewise, more junior employees must be able to enjoy and respect the manager with whom they are paired.

2. **Set Clear Goals and Expectations**
    a. It would help to discuss your expectations for the relationship with your mentoring partner upfront. Ensure that you're both committed and your goals are aligned. What do you want to get out of the relationship? What specific skills do you like to learn? What knowledge, skills, and experience can you, the manager, provide? How and where will you meet?

3. **Work on Your Communication Skills**

    a. Let's be honest. Communicating with someone from a different generation can be challenging at times. That goes both ways. So, ensure that you're sensitive to the other person's communication preferences and needs.

4. **Be Tactful, Patient, and Open-Minded**
   a. Both you and your reverse mentoring partner must be open to learning from one another. That's the whole point. So, remain respectful and listen actively without any preconceived ideas.
   b. When it's your turn to mentor, use constructive feedback to help your mentee understand your perspective and never blame, shame, or criticize. Be constructive with your tough feedback.

5. **Measure Your Progress**
   a. Check in regularly to ensure that you are both happy with the relationship and get the necessary information. However, if you are not progressing, schedule a brainstorming session and discuss new ways to achieve your goals.

Benefits of Curiosity

Research has found that curious people are known for having better relationships, and other people are more easily attracted and feel socially closer to individuals who display curiosity. Imagine what that will do to working relationships with employees, colleagues, customers, and other stakeholders. In one study, participants were asked to engage in intimate or small talk with other participants whom they had never met before. After having these conversations, researchers found that more curious people felt closer to their partners in conversations. Those who were less curious did not experience this same connection. When you show genuine curiosity toward others and ask questions, they open up and share more about themselves. They may also become curious about you and ask you questions. This creates a positive cycle of give and take, ultimately fostering closeness.[25]

Organizations can reap numerous benefits by hiring employees who display curiosity and promoting those employees into leadership roles.

Research conducted by Harvard Business School's Francesca Gino, a behavioral scientist, found that when our curiosity is stimulated, we are less likely to make mistakes in decision making. This is because when we are curious, we are less likely to be influenced by confirmation bias, where we tend to look for information that supports our beliefs rather than looking for evidence that suggests we may be incorrect. Similarly, we are less likely to stereotype people and make broad judgments, such as assuming that women or minorities do not make good leaders. This is because curiosity encourages us to generate alternatives and explore new perspectives.[26]

Gino's research also discovered that being curious can promote empathy among group members, encouraging them to take an interest in each other's ideas and perspectives rather than solely focusing on their own. This perspective-taking fosters more effective teamwork, resulting in smoother collaboration, less intense conflicts, and ultimately better outcomes.[27] Gino references another study by INSEAD's Spencer Harrison where the most curious employees tend to seek more information from their co-workers, and this information not only helps them perform better in their jobs but also enhances their creativity in addressing customers' concerns. Additionally, curious people in emotionally charged situations tend to respond less aggressively toward those who cause hurt feelings.[28]

The facts are laid out. Leaders who hire and promote curious employees will have more knowledgeable and higher-performing teams than teams that choose to remain siloed and closed off. Endless curiosity will only make teams better.

But what about individual leaders themselves? Is there a personal motivation for leaders to activate curiosity as a part of their daily routine?

Former *New York Times* "Corner Office" columnist Adam Bryant interviewed 525 chief executives and other leaders in a 10-year span and found that "applied curiosity" is the single most important quality that explains why they all became successful CEOs. So, what's behind applied curiosity? In Bryant's own words:

"It means trying to understand how things work, and then trying to understand how they can be made to work better. It means being curious about people and their backstories. It means using insights to build deceptively simple frameworks and models in their minds to make sense of their industry—and all the other disruptive forces shaping our world—so they can explain it to others. Then they continue asking questions about those models, and it's those questions that often lead to breakthrough ideas."[29]

Indeed, having an inquisitive mind is a valuable asset for any leader, and it comes with several advantages. The biggest may be continuous learning: A curious leader is always eager to learn to make informed decisions. They are open to change, willing to explore new strategies, and quick to pivot when necessary. This flexibility is crucial in today's dynamic business environment. But perhaps even more essential to learning is the courage to get honest about how others perceive the way you lead and do things.

Get Feedback, Get Better

In many organizations, as leaders climb the ranks and amass more power, there's a common tendency to become less open to listening to their employees. It's not uncommon for leaders to avoid candid discussions and steer clear of tough questions, fearing reactions that might challenge their authority. The fear extends to receiving feedback that could potentially tarnish their reputation, leading them to fiercely guard their privileged position.

Humble leaders, on the other hand, are willing to hold themselves accountable by seeking feedback and opening up channels of communication that promote organizational learning and improvement.

Self-Discovery Pitstop

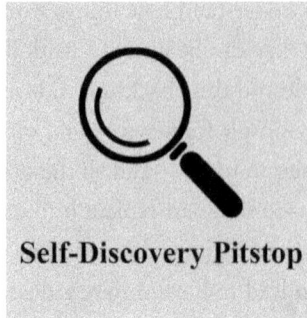

Feedback the Right Way
Start by seeking feedback from colleagues in low-pressure situations first and then gradually move up to higher stakes scenarios. You can start by asking, "I'm trying to understand how I'm perceived and the experiences I create for those who work with me. Can you give me some feedback on what I should continue doing, start doing, and stop doing?" Remember to focus on the positive aspects rather than just dwelling on the negative and what needs to be fixed.

When Jim Yong Kim was named the 12th president of the World Bank, he aimed to bring about significant changes in the organization's cultural and operational practices. The road was bumpy from the start, and he faced several daunting challenges. As he interacted with the employees, he asked them two questions: when were they proudest of being a World Bank employee, and what prevented them from being at their best every day?

The most common response he received was that the organization's culture was broken. To learn what was happening and address this issue, he conducted a survey and discovered a significant risk aversion within the company; employees were reluctant to take even the slightest risk for fear of losing their jobs. Additionally, there was a lack of trust within the organization, and the best managers and leaders were not being promoted. Communication between different divisions and regions was poor, and knowledge and insights were not shared.

Despite many people telling him that such large bureaucracies could never be changed, Kim refused to accept the idea that change was impossible. He sought to increase his learning by consulting with successful business leaders, such as Sam Palmisano (former CEO of

IBM) and Alan Mulally (former CEO of Ford Motor Company), who had achieved significant, well-publicized organizational changes. They emphasized the importance of communication and collaboration between employees and the breaking down of silos at all costs. Kim took the advice and set up meetings to review the entire business every two weeks, which had never been done before at the World Bank.

Kim eventually went on to be named one of the 100 most influential people in the world by *Time* magazine. He told a reporter from the *Washington Post,*

> No matter how good you think you are as a leader, my goodness, the people around you will have all kinds of ideas for how you can get better. So for me, the most fundamental thing about leadership is to have the humility to continue to get feedback and to try to get better.[30]

Kim changed the company from a rules-based bureaucracy to a strategically run, integrated organization by receiving feedback from global employees. He faced the ultimate reality that to achieve the company's goal of ending extreme poverty worldwide, the World Bank first had to change from the inside out by increasing their capacity to learn and grow, which precisely is what it did.

Stop Rewarding the Wrong Traits

At the beginning of this chapter, I posed a difficult question: why do we often witness egomaniacs and narcissists rise to the top of the corporate ladder, like Dan, my former CEO? I believe that this phenomenon is due to our flawed perception of what makes an effective leader.

Producing more humble leaders will require a systemic shift in our leadership selection processes and in our perception of what traits are worthy of reward and promotion.

What we *think* good leadership is actually far from the truth. Psychologist Tomas Chamorro-Premuzic points out that we've historically equated leadership with personality traits statistically more likely to be found in men: *confidence and charisma.*

In his book, *Why Do So Many Incompetent Men Become Leaders?* *(And How to Fix It)*, he sounds off the alarm by explaining how these same two characteristics can later backfire as overconfidence, narcissism, and even psychopathy, resulting in disaster.

Here's why you should not reward people—men or women alike—with the two masculine traits we have historically elevated as "leadership material" since the industrial age: confidence and charisma.

How Confidence Will Backfire

What Chamorro-Premuzic found is that when we perceive someone as confident, we naturally hire and promote that person to management. Based on his research findings, leaders are hired on confidence, and confident people—we've been conditioned to think and believe —tend to be more charismatic, extroverted, and socially skilled. In most Western cultures, these are highly desirable features we want in management roles.

Here's why so many companies ultimately fail under such leaders: we equate confidence with *competence*. Therefore, we automatically assume that confident people are also more able-skilled, that confident people are more talented, that confident people have what it takes to lead a company or a team, and we put our faith and trust in confident and charismatic leaders that, we falsely believe, will drive results and take us to the promised land. And many of them do, in fact. They can be great strategy people, visionaries, and movers and shakers who will do whatever it takes to succeed.

Here's the kicker: The reality is that competent people are generally confident, but confident people are *not necessarily* competent. So, you'll find that many confident leaders are good at hiding their incompetence and their insecurities—mainly because they think that they are much better than they actually are.

This is where disaster happens. Confidence can lead to overconfidence; it backfires as people in charge begin to show their true colors. You'll see arrogance, an ego that doesn't fit the room you're standing in, impulsive behavior, and narcissism, which will now destroy team dynamics, morale, collaboration, and productivity.

Let me put it to you this way: If you were interviewing someone for a high-level management role and you didn't have hard evidence or information on that person's actual leadership competence, but you "heard over the grapevine" that this person is a charismatic leader with executive presence, you would assume that they must be good leaders because they command a conversation and say all the right things, show "type A" tendencies, exude confident body language, and light up a room when they waltz in. Therefore, we tend to rely on these confident signs to make our hiring decisions. However, the real goal we should focus on is always—*always*—to understand how *competent* somebody is as a leader, and not how confident they appear to be.

"Decades of research suggest that on virtually any dimension of ability, we tend to assume that we are better than we actually are," Chamorro-Premuzic shared with me.[31] To his point, competence is how good you are at something, just like a heart surgeon having performed numerous triple bypasses before someone is willing to have their chest sliced open and their breastbone split down the middle. Confidence is how good you *think* you are at something, and it can be deceiving for both sides of the table. Although confidence is desirable, overconfident leaders tend to overestimate their abilities and job performance, leading to reckless decision making later. This is because they are less receptive to negative feedback as they move up the proverbial corporate ladder.

How Charisma Will Backfire

Some of the most successful leaders in the world are known for their charisma. But while charisma has been associated with extroversion, drive, and even more physically attractive features, it is hard to define and measure. Charisma exists in the eye of the beholder.

According to Chamorro-Premuzic, "Charisma clouds people's evaluations of how leaders actually perform. Rather than being objective, we are less judgmental about leaders' performance when we see them as charismatic, and we are more critical when we don't."[32]

In my own observations as an executive coach, behaviors of overconfidence and charisma escalate to arrogance and hubristic pride in destructive ways. For example:

- Arrogant leaders constantly show off their accomplishments or take credit for other people's work, thereby distancing themselves from others.
- They exaggerate because the simple truth doesn't get enough of a reaction.
- They serve in a leadership role to be noticed.
- They feel entitled to star treatment because of their position or title. Even more so when performing sacrificial work.
- They maneuver for a preferred position up the organizational chart.

The Mind of Humility

It's crucial to remember that the traits that propel more people into leadership roles are the same traits that get them fired. In other words, what we perceive as society's prerequisites for moving up the corporate ranks is the opposite of what it takes to lead exceptionally well.

According to Chamorro-Premuzic, while both male and female leaders are equal regarding IQ, studies show that women have greater emotional intelligence and, in general, perform better as leaders. Since a high degree of EQ is associated with the characteristics of humility, selecting and developing more leaders with humility traits—as competencies—would also help correct the gender imbalance in executive leadership ranks. Why? When humility is no longer overlooked as a leadership trait in our society, promoting individuals to high-ranking leadership positions will lead to more diversity and gender equality at the top. By recognizing the importance of humility in leadership, we can shift our culture toward a more inclusive and diverse leadership landscape.

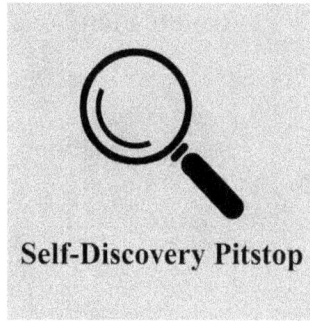

Self-Discovery Pitstop

The Humility Test

Circle the number corresponding to how frequently you think you have exhibited these self-centered attitudes within the last month. Add your total at the bottom.

1 = never *2* = rarely *3* = sometimes *4* = frequently

1 2 3 4 I boast about successes without crediting others.

1 2 3 4 I deserve special treatment because of my status or position.

1 2 3 4 I stretch the truth to get attention or be correct.

1 2 3 4 I micromanage others to ensure they do things my way.

1 2 3 4 I won't accommodate opinions or ideas different than my own.

1 2 3 4 I reject help from others, preferring to go it alone.

1 2 3 4 I have a hard time admitting to being wrong.

1 2 3 4 I have a hard time admitting if I don't know something.

1 2 3 4 I tend to seek out points of disagreement and engage in arguments.

1 2 3 4 I get annoyed easily and lash out at those who bother me.

Scoring Scale:

1–10 You are a model of a humble leader.

11–20 You are learning and on the right track to be more humble.

21–30 Thank you for your honesty. That's the first step to growing in humility.

31–40 There's work to be done and professional help may be needed.

Action Plan

Use this action plan to apply intellectual humility and humble leadership in your working relationships and professional development. Then, teach others to do the same to shape and embed humility into the DNA of your organization.

Action Item 1: Give Your People a Voice

Show that you value your employees by coming to them first to ask for input and advice on strategy and decisions that affect them on the front lines.

Action Item 2: Make It Safe to Talk About Mistakes

Mistakes are growth opportunities. Effective leaders acknowledge and learn from them openly and earn trust and respect. By embracing the lessons they provide, they can pave the way for better paths forward. Follow three rules to guide your team to learn from mistakes: (1) give them stretch assignments, (2) let them know you expect some mistakes, and (3) create space to learn from those mistakes.

Action Item 3: Activate Curiosity and Gather Feedback

Choose open-mindedness and curiosity to learn and improve over protecting your point of view. Laszlo Bock, CEO and cofounder of Humu, recommends sending an email to your team containing these three questions for feedback:

- What is one thing I currently do that you'd like me to continue to do?
- What is one thing that I don't currently do frequently enough that you think I should do more often?
- What can I do to make you more effective?[33]

Asking for feedback is a powerful way to improve and sets an example for others to follow. If you habitually ask for feedback, your team members will feel more comfortable doing the same. To take this to the next level, try scheduling in-person meetings to discuss the feedback you receive. This will help you build stronger connections and create an environment of trust and openness.

CHAPTER 6

Leadership Advocates for People

When you get these jobs you have been so brilliantly trained for, just remember that your real job is that if you are free, you need to free somebody else. If you have some power, then your job is to empower somebody else. This is not just a grab-bag candy game.

—Toni Morrison

The workplace has historically been a place for unfair treatment and injustices. Now, with AI playing a significant role in all areas of business—even in leadership—people worry about the potential for discrimination if AI adopts prejudiced strategies and unfairly treats certain groups. In a survey of over 600 employees across industries, when Potential Project researchers asked people if they were worried about using AI to make management decisions about hiring, promotions, and work assignments based on its understanding of human behavior, 69 percent said they had concerns.[1]

As we move toward an exciting AI-driven future full of possibilities, today's leaders must look at the possibilities of developing caring human leadership skills with equal excitement and dedication. Right now, AI cannot match or perform one honorable Love in Action leadership principle that humans possess: advocating for others.

Advocacy on behalf of other people is a fundamental aspect of effective leadership in the 21st century. Today's workforce looks and thinks differently from the *Ally McBeal* or *The Office* generations before them. In my parents' generation, workers got what was given to them, took their marching orders, clocked in and out, and didn't complain. It was a transactional experience of trading skills for a paycheck, with no emotional attachment or engagement required. Fast forward to 2020, and we found that the pandemic disrupted our work lives in a myriad of ways. It led 65 percent of workers to reconsider the role of work in their lives, while 52 percent questioned the purpose of their jobs.[2]

Owing to workforce shortages and dramatically changed workplace attitudes, today's workers are more agile, resourceful, and empowered than ever. Since the workforce no longer looks or acts the same as it did two decades ago or even five years ago, leading it the same way makes as much sense as teaching a fish to ride a bicycle.

Making Things Right

To adapt to the new world of work, we need to evolve the leadership mindset that advocates for a fair, just, and inclusive workforce. Let's be clear, though. The Love in Action principle of advocacy is multifaceted, but ultimately translates to "righting the wrongs." Leaders who advocate stand their ground in defending and protecting their people, especially during crises and challenging times and transitions. Drawing from the original root word from the Greek—*Stego*—this principle found in the Corinthians account means "to cover or to support and therefore to protect." In paraphrasing, it's about making things right. In the volatile and politically charged 21st century, leaders make things right by protecting others from institutional harm and firmly standing up to and against corruption, harassment, favoritism, racism, chauvinism, inequality, "fast firings," and other unethical corporate shenanigans. The benefit of advocacy reinforces strong community and collaboration for business outcomes and ultimately supports the values of actionable love.

Richard Sheridan, CEO of Menlo Innovations, is a strong leader-advocate who believes in preserving, protecting, and defending his company's culture and people. In his book *Chief Joy Officer*, Sheridan highlights the leadership of co-CEOs of Next Jump Associates, Charlie Kim and Meghan Messenger, who have a "never fire anyone" rule. Once employees receive the Next Jump jacket, their peers commit to preserving, protecting, and defending them even if they are not performing well. The team takes ownership of each other as if they were family. In 2012, Next Jump shifted from letting go of the bottom 10 percent of performers to not firing anyone.

Next Jump's hiring process involves multiple interactions to ensure a good fit. As a result, every hiring manager started hiring more carefully, treating hiring like adoption. Once someone is hired, they are part of the Next Jump family for life. If things don't work out, the team takes responsibility for training and helping the employee. Training also became more comprehensive, covering character, grit, and integrity, previously viewed as beyond the scope of company training.

Sheridan notes that Bob Chapman, CEO of Barry–Wehmiller, has reinforced the idea of hiring being like adoption and employees being considered family. Bob and Charlie discussed Charlie's original practice of "fast firing" to end a bad fit quickly. Bob asked Charlie how he would feel if he heard his son was fired from a job. Charlie realized that a firing is equivalent to someone important in your life telling you, "You're no good." If he didn't want that for his son, why would he want that for his team members?

Sheridan emphasizes that protection is not only crucial during times of economic abundance but also during scarcity. Next Jump Associates and Barry-Wehmiller were at risk during the dotcom bust and 2008 financial crisis. Sheridan writes,

> It is always easy to imagine being a great leader during times of abundance, but our value as leaders is only put to the test when hard times hit. When those hard times hit us, we must show love to keep moving forward. And ... our teams will be looking for us to keep them energized about the future, no matter the present situation.[3]

To advocate well, I'll provide you with a roadmap broken down into three practical components that can be emulated and replicated across any organization:

1. Believe in people.
2. Protect people's mental health and well-being.
3. Right the wrongs.

Believe the Best in People

Believing in people before they have proved themselves is the key to motivating people to reach their potential.

—John C. Maxwell

In the hustle of daily tasks and endless meetings, it's easy for leaders to spend days, months, or even years alongside their teams without really connecting. It's like an invisible barrier that keeps us from truly understanding our team members' growth needs or recognizing their unique strengths. But then, something almost magical happens when we start making a conscious effort to connect—be it through praise, a genuine smile, or a brief chat to steer someone in the right direction.

Suddenly, that barrier we didn't even know existed begins to crumble. It's in these moments that we start to forge real connections. The fears that once loomed large—being fully present, showing our true selves, and truly seeing others—start to dissipate. We embark on a journey of mutual trust and respect by choosing to believe in the best of those around us.

You'll recall Bruce—the best boss I ever worked for from Chapter 2—as a shining example of a loving leader who connected with his team. Soon after he hired me, Bruce began exposing me to high-level activities, such as placing me in the chairperson role of an executive council of community leaders for a multimillion-dollar project. At that time, I had no business being in that role and was terrified. But Bruce saw something in me that I didn't: he believed in my ability to grow in that area and provided the initial handholding to get me through the humps until I mastered the role and shined in it.

Advocating for people entails choosing to see the best in them. A good leader opts for trust and optimism instead of immediately doubting their actions. Rather than assuming that "they're beyond improvement," Love in Action means holding onto hope and believing in someone's growth potential.

To believe in someone means we must also acknowledge that people do have weak spots and will make mistakes. Instead of giving them the immediate shaft, we must recognize each individual's capacity for positive change. Instead of rushing to judgment with cynicism and suspicion, Love in Action leadership maintains faith in the inherent goodness of each team member, believing in their ability to learn, grow, and improve. Every situation presents an opportunity for leaders to demonstrate empathy and support, encouraging their team members to reach their full potential.

People Can and Will Change

A great illustration of this premise comes from the penal system. In 2005, the Bureau of Justice Statistics studied recidivism in state prisoners. The study tracked former inmates from 30 states for five years after release. The results showed that an estimated two-thirds (68 percent) of the 405,000 prisoners who were released in those 30 states were arrested for a new crime within three years of being released from prison. Additionally, three-quarters (77 percent) were arrested within five years. More than a third (37 percent) of those arrested within five years of being released were arrested within the first six months, and more than half (57 percent) were arrested by the end of the first year.[4]

You may be thinking that it's pointless to believe in the potential of released criminals and hope that they can change and reintegrate into society. Just look at those stats again. However, not everybody sees the glass half empty. Dr. Mimi Halper Silbert founded a program called Delancey Street in San Francisco, which provides residential rehabilitation services and vocational training programs for convicted criminals.

The average Delancey Street resident has had 12 years of drug addiction, has been in prison four times, is functionally illiterate, unskilled, and has never worked for more than six months. "People who have become involved with gangs, drugs, violence, crime ... those are our favorite residents," Silbert said.[5] Residents of Delancey Street who successfully complete the program acquire a range of skills, including vocational, personal, interpersonal, and social skills. These skills allow individuals to make amends to society for their past criminal behavior.

Graduates of the program who were initially functionally illiterate and unemployed have gone on to earn bachelor's degrees, establish careers, and secure jobs at various successful businesses owned by Delancey Street. These businesses include moving and trucking companies, cafes and bookstores, event planning and catering services, and art galleries.

Nearly 60 percent of people who participate in the program complete it and go on to lead productive lives. Compared to the traditional penal system, this level of transformation is quite impressive: 6 out of 10 individuals thriving in life versus 6 out of 10 who end up returning to crime and subsequently being sent back to prison.

Dr. Silbert has achieved remarkable results by creating an environment that fosters the belief that even criminals can change. When these former inmates and recovering addicts are met with love and acceptance and offered a second chance, they become accountable and transformed beyond measure. Dr. Silbert's approach emphasizes a powerful message: Collective belief can have a significant impact.

The Workplace Application

How do you come to know and believe in someone? It usually begins with a fleeting glimmer of potential that you see in them, as Bruce did in me. To recognize this potential, you must believe in them and be curious about their abilities. It would help if you enjoyed observing whether someone can develop, improve, and excel.

Evidence suggests that leaders' beliefs in others can create self-fulfilling prophecies in the workplace. A meta-analysis of 17 different studies involving nearly 3,000 employees revealed a significant correlation: When managers perceived their employees as having high potential, those employees tended to thrive. This "Pygmalion effect"— a psychological term for self-fulfilling prophecy—suggests that having higher expectations leads to an increase in performance. Researchers encourage managers to recognize the power of genuinely believing in their employees' potential and take actions supporting and communicating this belief. By doing so, managers can increase their employees' motivation and effort, ultimately helping them realize their full potential.

In my experience coaching managers and executives, I see two perspectives: On the one hand, many of my clients believe in their people and don't wait for signs of potential. They naturally see people as "bloomers" without being reminded. Because they tend to be trusting and optimistic about other people's intentions, they are inclined to see the potential in everyone.

On the other hand, I've worked with leaders whose distrust in their people often leads to negative results. Because of their suspicion that people, especially younger generations, are self-serving, entitled, and only looking after themselves, they tend to hold low expectations for the potential of others.

Studies support the idea that managers who are suspicious of their team members' intentions, even if those intentions are positive, will constantly monitor them for signs of wrongdoing. This leads to a toxic work environment of distrust, ultimately hindering team members' growth and motivation.[6]

Spotting Potential in Others

Throughout this book, I've stressed the centrality of love as a means to lead people effectively, which benefits both the leader and the people entrusted under their care. Love of people—a prerequisite for leadership—is the only way to grasp another human being's potential. To quote Viktor Frankl in *Man's Search for Meaning*,

> No one can become fully aware of the very essence of another human being unless he loves him. By his love he is enabled to see the essential traits and features in the beloved person; and even more, he sees that which is potential in him, which is not yet actualized but yet ought to be actualized. Furthermore, by his love, the loving person enables the beloved person to actualize these potentialities. By making him aware of what he can be and of what he should become, he makes these potentialities come true.

Believe in the Greatest Good Possible

Imagine if our workplaces were seen as hubs of realized potential, the places people could point to as the one area in their lives where they were growing and developing. Unfortunately, this is rarely the case today. This may be why so much data indicates that employees don't feel empowered or developed by their leaders. We, as leaders, work off the talent management playbook and try all the techniques that coaches and consultants throw at us to help people reach their full potential, except the one that has been proven to work: *love*.

Eventually, we must stop spinning our wheels and learn to have faith in a greater good that is within reach for every individual. But what exactly is this "greatest good"? I'll answer that with another question: How would you describe what you desire most for the people you love using just one word?

For me, it's *flourishing*. The word "flourishing" encompasses the greatest good and represents the ultimate goal for those we care about. It all starts with the belief that there is a greatest good possible for every person we serve. Without this belief, there is little to care for, to challenge, and to develop. Love in Action is about discovering each person's untapped potential, imagining the ways they can succeed, and bulldozing a clear path ahead for them to flourish as human beings.

Whenever you help people actualize their potential and fulfill their felt needs, you are "unveiling the masterpiece from the canvas." Just as a beautiful painting emerges from a blank canvas through an artist's skill and effort, great achievements in people can emerge from seemingly small beginnings with nurturing, belief, and advocacy. It's working with them, coaching and mentoring them, having career-development conversations with them, and ultimately bringing out their best selves.

Put Your Hope in Others

Always remember that indifference, suspicion, and bias believe the worst in people; Love in Action believes the best. As long as there is hope for others, human failure is never final. In hope, there is a desire in a leader's heart to believe that something will change and that a person will turn around. And when things go wrong and you lose hope, hope some more. Love in Action keeps encouraging, keeps building up, and refuses to take failure as final. It cares too much to give up.

By giving love to others along the journey, our advocacy can be a driving force for good in the way we lead teams and organizations. You have the ability to shape your own experience. Lead with advocacy and watch your own influence and leadership bloom.

LeadershipToolbox

Four Steps to Identify Someone's True Potential
1. Observe their talents and strengths and notice where they excel with little effort on specific tasks.
2. Learn about someone's interests to give you a window into their passions and dreams, revealing their natural inclinations.
3. Pay attention to people's values. Notice what they'll go to great lengths to protect, what they truly cherish, and what speaks to their identity. By understanding their personal value system, you'll be better equipped to lead them in a way that motivates and inspires them.
4. Understand people's personal stories, defining moments, and proud accomplishments. These things can provide insights into a person's actual potential.

Protect Their Mental Health and Well-Being

Your mental health is everything–prioritize it. Make the time like your life depends on it, because it does.

—Mel Robbins

When Steve Jobs introduced the original iPhone during an unforgettable product launch at MacWorld in 2007, the world was changed forever. It was never Jobs's intent, but something tragic and unexpected happened when smartphones began ruling our lives: We became, and are still becoming, increasingly detached, isolated, and relationally agnostic.

Contrary to the illusion that today's workers are highly connected to one another through their devices, most people actually feel isolated from their colleagues, and the main cause of social isolation is technology itself.

In his book *Back to Human: How Great Leaders Create Connection in the Age of Isolation*, Dan Schawbel argues that most people feel isolated from their colleagues. Schawbel interviewed 100 top young leaders, and most agreed that their devices are a "double-edged sword" in that they help their teams become superconnected but at the cost of the human touch.

The Loneliness Epidemic

Vivek Murthy, who has served as the 19th and 21st surgeon general of the United States, declared overall loneliness, isolation, and lack of connection in our country as a public health crisis. Even before the pandemic, approximately half of U.S. adults reported experiencing measurable levels of loneliness, increasing the risk for individuals to develop mental health challenges. Additionally, Murthy said that "lacking social connection increases (the) risk of premature death by more than 60 percent."

"Our epidemic of loneliness and isolation has been an underappreciated public health crisis that has harmed individual and societal health," Murthy said in a statement.[7] To counter loneliness and isolation, the solution is quite simple and even more critical in postpandemic times.

"Our relationships are a source of healing and well-being hiding in plain sight—one that can help us live healthier, more fulfilled, and more productive lives," said Murthy.

Affirming Murthy's statement, one global study found that what people at work crave the most is a sense of authentic human connection with others. In most cases, though, technology can make the workplace more dysfunctional. It keeps employees constantly working, even after they "leave the office," leading to burnout and other health problems. (One-third of the more than 2,000 employees surveyed for this prepandemic study worked remotely.[8]) In Cigna's 2019 study of 10,441 working adults in the United States, three in five reported that they are lonely. The same survey revealed that, on average, lonely employees think about quitting their jobs more than twice as often as nonlonely workers.[9]

Things moved in much the same trajectory during the height of the pandemic and the so-called Great Resignation. One national survey found that 36 percent of U.S. adults experienced serious loneliness— feeling lonely "frequently" or "almost all the time or all the time," including an astounding 61 percent of young people aged 18 to 25.[10]

While citizens and government alike did their part, and rightfully so, to slow the spread of COVID-19 by instituting lockdowns and social distancing, the workforce was suddenly forced to be alone, cut off from the social networks and work communities that their places of employment provided. It was a collective shock to the system—the organizational system and the emotional system of the average worker.

While many attribute this crisis to the pandemic and the belief that as people returned to in-person interaction, the feeling would resolve itself, the problem isn't just that people feel isolated but also that many companies lack strong connections and community within their workforces. Murthy stresses this point clearly: "Given the significant health consequences of loneliness and isolation, we must prioritize building social connection the same way we have prioritized other critical public health issues such as tobacco, obesity, and substance use disorders."

If we want to increase the mental and emotional well-being of people in the workplace, decision makers at the highest levels must advocate for people's mental health. Our social connections are the power source of our well-being, and those connections must be continuously nurtured where we spend the majority of our awake time outside the home.

Increase Prosocial Behaviors at Work

Decreasing loneliness by establishing meaningful connections at work takes a lot less effort than one might think. According to psychologists, the best way to lessen loneliness and limit its effects is by using "prosocial behaviors" that include actions of comforting, sharing, helping, or cooperating that are backed by a general concern for the feelings, welfare, and rights of other people.[11]

Loneliness is contagious, but so are prosocial actions like mutually helping one another at work. In studies, those on the receiving end of prosocial behaviors were a whopping 278 percent as likely to engage in prosocial behaviors themselves.[12] The ripple effect of positive behaviors is gigantic. If you routinely extend kindness and help your peers and colleagues, it will ignite similar behaviors throughout your organization and even to the broader world, leading to a healthier you, stronger families, and more united communities, which the world desperately needs right now. This requires businesses and organizations to stop relying on cutthroat, high-pressure, take-no-prisoners work settings.

Address Proximity Bias

Prosocial behaviors are even more necessary in remote work environments. In early 2020, remote work seemed like the dream setup for many: comfy clothes all day, no commutes, and frequent trips to the fridge.

Yet, recent research reveals a significant challenge for those embracing full-time remote work: career advancement. According to an analysis by Live Data Technologies, which looked at two million white-collar workers, remote employees were promoted 31 percent less often than their counterparts who worked from the office, whether full-time or in a hybrid model. Additionally, remote workers, particularly women, receive less mentorship, highlighting a crucial area for improvement in remote work dynamics.[13]

Studies have shown that those working fully remotely are more productive than their on-site counterparts. However, remote workers often miss out on building solid relationships due to the lack of social interactions and in-person conversations, affecting their chances of getting promoted. Researchers who study remote work and management practices state that there's some proximity bias among the challenges facing remote workers. One prominent scholar told *Wall Street*, "I literally call it discrimination."[14]

Work Less Hours

One powerful way to advocate for people's mental health is to challenge conventional views of how many hours we think people must work to be productive and, instead, trust them to make good choices with their schedule that will benefit them and the organization.

Plenty of evidence suggests that the 9-to-5 workday may soon become extinct. I say this because the standard eight-hour workday was established during the Industrial Revolution when assembly line work was the norm. Henry Ford, observing his production line more than a century ago, noticed that workplace accidents increased significantly after the ninth hour of work. As a result, to reduce accidents and increase productivity, he limited the work shift to eight hours. Thus, the concept of the eight-hour workday was born out of the realities of manual labor.[15] Over time, as more companies bowed down to the gods of profit and productivity, 8-hour workdays in the knowledge economy voluntarily increased to 10, 12, or longer across industries as a badge of honor and cultural expectation of loyalty to those in the chain of command. But as I mentioned in Chapter 1, it also increased mortality by almost 20 percent.[16]

To advocate for less human suffering and increased well-being, the simple solution is deconstructing how we work. We really don't need that many hours to be productive; we don't even need five *workdays* per week. In a 2016 survey of nearly 2,000 full-time office workers in the United Kingdom, nearly 80 percent of respondents said they were productive for an average of just 2 hours and 53 minutes per day.[17] In a study of about 5,000 employees published in Morten Hansen's book, *Great at Work*, Hansen found that performance is not directly related to the number of hours worked. Hansen's final conclusion: the more hours worked, the lower the productivity per hour worked.[18]

A study conducted in Iceland, with about 1 percent of the country's workforce, showed that working fewer hours can be more beneficial to health and productivity. The workers cut out three to five hours from their work week without any reduction in pay but maintained their productivity levels and experienced improvements in their overall well-being. The study was so successful that almost 85 percent of Icelanders have since worked a four-day workweek.[19]

Microsoft Japan experimented with a four-day work week in August of 2019, giving its 2,300 employees five Fridays off in a row without any pay cuts. The result? A 40 percent boost in productivity, happier employees, and more efficient meetings. "Work a short time, rest well, and learn a lot," Microsoft Japan president and CEO Takuya Hirano said. "I want employees to think about and experience how they can achieve the same results with 20 percent less working time."[20]

These studies indicate that leaders should trust their teams' abilities to complete their work without the unrealistic demands that jeopardize people's health and well-being. They'll still get a productive work environment but, more importantly, a more fulfilling work experience for their employees.

I argue that compelling individuals to work 50-plus hours a week is inhumane. The argument isn't about giving them more time for family or leisure activities or less time for work (although that's a clear benefit); it's about having a well-balanced and holistic lifestyle to improve their quality of life. The primary objective here is to provide exceptional care to people because it's the right and loving thing to do.

Right the Wrongs

The secret to success is good leadership, and good leadership is all about making the lives of your team members or workers better.

—Tony Dungy

Tesla and X (formerly Twitter) chief executive Elon Musk may not be the poster child for Love in Action that inspires loyalty and commitment—far from it, in fact, after reports that he fired over 80 percent of Twitter before purchasing the social media giant—but he has shown rare flashes of fairness and advocacy that garnered media attention.

In 2017, a report by Worksafe, a worker advocacy group based in California, pointed out that the injury rates at Tesla's Fremont manufacturing facility were more than 30 percent higher than the industry average in 2014 and 2015.[21] When Musk learned of the many injuries at the plant, his humanity sprang into action. In one heartfelt email to Tesla employees, which was leaked to the public, he included this message:

> No words can express how much I care about your safety and well-being. It breaks my heart when someone is injured building cars and trying their best to make Tesla successful. Going forward, I've asked that every injury be reported directly to me, without exception. I'm meeting with the safety team every week and would like to meet every injured person as soon as they are well, so that I can understand from them exactly what we need to do to make it better. I will then go down to the production line and perform the same task that they perform. This is what all managers at Tesla should do as a matter of course. At Tesla, we lead from the front line, not from some safe and comfortable ivory tower. Managers must always put their team's safety above their own.[22]

It would be challenging for Musk to ensure the safety of over 10,000 people working at Tesla's Fremont factory, as accidents are inevitable at some point. But more to the point, Musk highlights the importance of managers getting directly involved in their team's work instead of creating distance from them. Learning firsthand about what's happening on the frontlines and with your own employees is essential to fixing problems and righting the wrongs.

Addressing safety issues at a manufacturing plant is only one spoke of the wheel in corporate wrongdoing. As more narcissists rising to positions of power and influence are exposed, we are faced with an ever-growing crisis: the absence of ethical leaders who value the dignity of *all* human beings at work.

The Gender Pay Gap

According to the American Association of University Women (AAUW), U.S. Census Bureau data from 2023 revealed that women working full time, on average, make 84 cents compared to every dollar men make. AAUW's research shows that certain groups of women face significant pay inequities as compared to white, non-Hispanic men. The pay gap is the widest for Latina women workers, who earn just 52 cents for every dollar earned by white, non-Hispanic men. Black women workers earn 66 cents for every dollar, and white women workers earn 74 cents for every dollar. Asian American women workers fare slightly better, earning 89 cents for every dollar white, non-Hispanic men earn.[23]

While many tech companies, including Google, Twitter, Microsoft, and Uber, have found themselves in class-action gender-discrimination suits over the last decade,[24] the leader of the future is the one who examines gender pay gaps and says, "We will not tolerate that here."

One such leader is Salesforce CEO Marc Benioff. The San Francisco-based cloud computing company chief continues to level the playing field regarding pay equality, but it was Salesforce's former chief people officer, Cindy Robbins, and her colleague, former executive vice president (VP) Leyla Seka, who first raised the issue of a pay gap between men and women at Salesforce. An audit had uncovered a statistical difference in pay between men and women.

"We wanted to figure out what we could do to help other women at Salesforce," said Robbins. They courageously brought the pay gap to Benioff's attention in 2015, who was at first stunned and in denial but quickly stepped up to fix what would be a $6 million problem. "It was everywhere," Benioff admitted in a *60 Minutes* interview.[25] "It was through the whole company, every department, every division, every geography." Benioff fixed the problem by dedicating $3 million that year to correct the discrepancy, another $3 million in 2017 to correct compensation differences by gender, race, and ethnicity across the company, and another $2.7 million in 2018 to close pay gaps to adjust the salaries of 6 percent of its global 30,000-person workforce.[26] As of March 2023, Salesforce has invested more than $12 million to evaluating and improving their pay practices.[27]

He also created a new rule that would increase the likelihood of women being promoted and seen as leaders. "We would have a meeting and I would look around the room and I'm like, 'This meeting is just men. Something is not right,'" he told *60 Minutes*. So, he announced he would not hold a meeting unless 30 percent of the participants were women.

"There's No Excuse"

More executives at the helm of companies like Salesforce are being intentional about eliminating gender bias by implementing clear policies and guidelines against gender pay gaps and making sure salaries are regularly reviewed for gender parity.

And that's what makes Benioff stand out. He believes you can't be a decent CEO if you're not committed to gender equality. In his campaign to raise awareness, he's had to convince plenty of other male executives of its importance and that the problem of a pay gap *actually does exist*.

"I've had CEOs call me and say, 'This is not true. This is not real,'" he told *60 Minutes*. "And I'll say to them, 'This *is* true. Look at the numbers.'"

"CEOs, with one button on one computer, can pay every man and every woman equally," he adds. "We have the data. We know what everyone makes. There's no excuse."[28]

It's inspiring to see how Salesforce, under Benioff's leadership, has taken a strong stance on equality, both within its own workforce and in the communities it serves. The company is an ardent advocate for gender, LGBTQ, racial, national origin, and religious equality. It's heartening to witness how Salesforce is working toward building a more inclusive and equitable future for all.

Leaders must intentionally eliminate bias by ensuring that their hiring and promotion practices have clear policies and guidelines against it and that there are checks and balances in place where salaries between genders are regularly reviewed for parity.

Promote More Women Into Leadership Roles

The issue goes much deeper into systemic and cultural roots. Until leaders and managers crush the toxic power values of misogynistic work cultures and male-white privilege, we'll continue to witness inexcusable injustices such as sexual harassment and the gender pay gap.

Research shows that harassment is more common in workplaces where men hold most managerial jobs. This is because male-dominated management teams may sometimes overlook or even encourage sexualized behavior toward employees, creating an environment that tolerates harassment where inappropriate actions are ignored or laughed off instead of being confronted. Women who are harassed might be ostracized, feeling ashamed for not speaking up. And those who do speak up are often punished for doing so. To improve this, reducing power imbalances is crucial in decreasing sexual harassment for the simple proven fact that women in management roles not only tend to avoid harassment but also positively influence workplace culture.[29]

The solution to these problems is quite simple: Hire and promote more women into leadership roles who will, in turn, create a positive and safe work environment for everyone.

This, however, is an uphill battle. Back in 2015, McKinsey & Company teamed up with LeanIn.Org to study women's roles in corporate America and equip companies with the insights and tools they need to boost gender diversity at work. From 2015 to 2023, the "Women in the Workplace" initiative (which includes cisgender and transgender women) has seen participation from over 900 companies and more than 450,000 individuals about their experiences on the job. In 2023 alone, researchers surveyed over 27,000 employees from 276 organizations and held interviews with a diverse group, including women of color, LGBTQ + women, and women with disabilities, to get a well-rounded view of the landscape.[30]

First, the good news. Since 2015, the presence of women in the C-suite has climbed from 17 to 28 percent, and there's been a notable uptick in the number of women at the VP and SVP levels too. This progress is definitely worth a round of applause. However, despite these gains, an uncomfortable truth persists: women, particularly women of color, are still underrepresented across all levels in corporate America.[31]

The Broken Rung

The term "glass ceiling" has been around for over four decades, spotlighting that invisible barrier that keeps women from climbing to the top ranks in their careers. The data points to a much bigger and earlier hurdle at the first major leap toward becoming a manager.

In 2023, out of every 100 men who stepped up from entry-level positions to management roles, only 87 women made the same leap. The situation looks even more challenging for women of color: only 73 got promoted for every 100 men, a drop from 82 in 2022. The numbers are particularly stark for early-career Black women. Their promotion rates, which had improved to 82 and 96 for every 100 men in 2020 and 2021—likely due to increased attention to diversity, equity, and inclusion issues—have regrettably slipped back to 2019's low of 54 for every 100 men promoted.[32]

As a result of this broken rung, women fall behind and can't catch up. The disparity continues throughout careers as men move up the ladder in larger numbers and make up the lion's share of outside hires.

Supporting Employees of Color

We can't forget about racial diversity. There are more people with more diverse backgrounds working than ever before. Leaders must advocate for Black, Indigenous, and people of color populations at work by encouraging prevailing groups to engage with people outside their race. Employees must step out of their comfort zone and stretch themselves to talk with people who grew up in different places, believe different things, look differently, and live and worship differently than they do. They need to talk with them, listen to them, and get their perspectives about things that matter in the workplace.

If financial metrics are important to you, research supports the business case for more diversity. A 2015 McKinsey study on 366 public companies found that those in the top quartile for ethnic and racial diversity in management were 35 percent more likely to have financial returns above their industry mean, and those in the top quartile for gender diversity were 15 percent more likely to have returns above the industry mean.[33] Moreover, one study of 177 U.S. banks found that a racially diverse workforce was related to enhanced financial performance in banks with an innovation-focused business strategy.[34]

Myths, Realities, and Allies

Some argue that women are less ambitious, leading to their lower representation in leadership roles. This is a myth. Women today are as ambitious as ever, equally committed to their careers, and just as eager for promotions as men. At the director level, where the C-suite becomes a tangible goal, both women and men show the same level of interest in climbing the leadership ladder. Young women, in particular, are highly driven: 90 percent aim for the next level, and 75 percent aspire to senior leadership positions. The pandemic and the shift toward more flexible work arrangements haven't quelled this ambition. About 80 percent of women are aiming for a promotion this year (2024), up from 70 percent in 2019—a trend mirrored by men.[35]

Despite the numbers staring us in the face, progress is like pushing a boulder uphill when you've got the old guard clinging to outdated views, especially in those traditionally white, male-dominated spots. They can't tackle issues they're blind to or refuse to see. This is exactly where both male and female *allies* in management who genuinely appreciate diversity's role in boosting team performance and business results come into play. These are the people who don't get swayed by politicized pressures or the noise of culture wars. They're the ones who'll really move the needle in lifting women up in the workplace.

Allies take it upon themselves to ensure that diversity isn't just a buzzword but a reality in how things work day-to-day. They're the ones who'll actually dig into the numbers, looking at who's being hired and who's moving up in the company, to make sure that everyone *who is qualified for the job* gets a fair shot.

We need more allies to advance diversity but for the right reasons. If multiplied throughout companies and across generations, we can collectively rebuild workplaces where individuals from all walks of life— future mothers, daughters, people of all racial and ethnic backgrounds, and members of the LGBTQ + community—can feel safe and truly proud of their contributions and advancement. There's a lot of love in that.

Action Plan

To start on the road to good leadership advocacy, the journey begins with a question for self-reflection: *Am I truly an advocate?* If you're unsure, how can you self-assess to ensure you are one?

The best way to challenge your assumptions and measure yourself against the high bar of leadership advocacy is to know how often you step in to help others—to remove roadblocks, ensure fairness, protect, lift up, and let people know, "I see you." The only way to find out is to go back to one of our earliest lessons: *Raise your self-awareness.* Your action item for this chapter is a list of questions you can have your team members anonymously answer about you, the leader or manager.

💡 Action Item: Nine Questions Your Team Members Should Be Asked

1. Does my manager take a stand against wrongdoing and proactively take steps against it?

2. Does my manager ensure that the voices of all team members, especially those from underrepresented groups, are heard and valued?

3. Does my manager advocate for fair compensation, benefits, and working conditions for team members?

4. Does my manager address and challenge workplace bias, discrimination, harassment, or inequity?

5. Does my manager prioritize the well-being and work–life balance of team members?

6. Does my manager take steps to foster a culture of trust, respect, and inclusivity within the team?

7. Does my manager advocate for flexibility and accommodation to support team members' diverse needs and responsibilities outside of work?

8. Does my manager stand up for our rights and interests in the face of organizational challenges or conflicts?

9. Does my manager actively involve team members in decision-making processes that affect their work and lives?

These questions can help you reflect on your leadership approach and identify areas where you can further advocate for your team members.

CHAPTER 7

Leadership Is Trustworthy

Trust is the lubrication that makes it possible for organizations to work.

—Warren Bennis

Billionaire investor Warren Buffett is known not only for his prolific investment acumen but also for his wisdom. One helpful tip that stood out for me came from his 2024 annual letter to shareholders. In an age of so much corporate wrongdoing, enormous egos, and horrific management decisions, it can be difficult to know whom to trust. Nearing a century of life, Buffett has seen the perils of human nature first-hand. Here's what he wrote as a warning for all of us:

> In 1863, Hugh McCulloch, the first Comptroller of the United States, sent a letter to all national banks. His instructions included this warning: "Never deal with a rascal under the expectation that you can prevent him from cheating you." Many bankers who thought they could "manage" the rascal problem have learned the wisdom of Mr. McCulloch's advice—and I have as well. People are not that easy to read. Sincerity and empathy can easily be faked. That is as true now as it was in 1863.

Beware of Rascals

Buffett relies on capable and trustworthy managers to run his Berkshire Hathaway-owned businesses. Still, it can be challenging to judge who's trustworthy and who's a bonafide "rascal."

In his 1989 annual letter to Berkshire Hathaway shareholders, the "Oracle of Omaha," as Buffet is known, called attention to a valuable personal rule that he credits with much of his success. He said,

"After some other mistakes, I learned to go into business only with people whom I like, trust, and admire." Later, he added, "We've never succeeded in making a good deal with a bad person."

There are always people looking to bend the rules, twist the truth, or manipulate an outcome to their advantage. That's just the world we live in. Buffett's point is that associating with these types of people is risky because, over time, you'll become more like them. As he puts it, "You want to associate with people who are the kind of person you'd like to be. You'll move in that direction."

Why Trustworthiness?

So, we bring Love in Action to its final tenet. Why end your journey with a chapter on trustworthiness? Getting back to the original context, in 1 Corinthians 13:7, we once again see that love is not just an abstract concept but an active force. Depending on which translation you read, one of those specific actions is that love "always trusts." Another translation is that love also "believes all things," which we covered in the last chapter by pointing out that leaders "believe the best in people." Granted, believing in all things does not make a leader gullible, a fool, or someone to be taken advantage of. None of those things are a part of love.

Digging a little deeper into the original language, "to believe" derives from the Greek word "pisteuo," which signifies "to trust" or "to have faith." These terms are often employed as expressions of love and illustrate the importance of trust and faith in human relationships, which is so drastically missing in this polarizing era of mistrust and suspicion.

We need to remember that trust is a two-way street. We can choose to trust and believe in others, but we must also show trustworthy behaviors for others to trust us, as leaders.

Trust Is Down

This is especially key in an age where trust is eroding rapidly. According to Gallup, trust in leadership has dropped since the pandemic began.

In 2022, only 21 percent of U.S. employees surveyed said that they trust their organization's leadership.[1] Trustworthiness is relevant because it links to the other tenets of Love In Action found in this book as the outcome of those learned traits and practices. But even so, when Patience, Kindness, Humility, and Advocacy are missing in action, we can lean on four practices—two that promote trust in others and two that develop a leader's trustworthiness:

1. Trust others: Extend trust first.
2. Trust others: Assume positive intent.
3. Become trustworthy: Lead selflessly.
4. Become trustworthy: Speak your truth.

Extend Trust First

When it comes to building trust, leaders go first.
            —Jim Kouzes and Barry Posner

In his book *The Speed of Trust*, Stephen M.R. Covey wrote that a team with high trust will produce results faster and at a lower cost. But should you first earn the trust of your people? Or does trust develop from having a belief in your people first—their strengths, abilities, and commitment?

In other words, which of these two statements would you agree with?

A. Trust is something that people must earn.

B. Trust is something that should be given as a gift.

If you chose A, you're in the majority. Conventional thinking says that people have to earn trust first before being granted special rights or privileges. If they violate that trust or royally mess up, it becomes difficult to earn it back. They may have to work twice as hard to prove themselves worthy of trust again. But if you selected B, pat yourself on the back. Covey found that, in high-performing organizations, leaders are willing to *give* trust to their followers first, and they give it as a gift even before it's earned.[2]

In 1994, well after Steve Jobs got booted by Apple and before returning to launch the iPad and iPhone revolution, he was interviewed by *Rolling Stone* magazine during one of the lowest points of his career. What ensued was a conversation that mostly covered topics around software development and the technological landscape of that era. And then this from Jobs:

> Technology is nothing. What's important is that you have a faith in people, that they're basically good and smart, and if you give them tools, they'll do wonderful things with them.

That answer was in response to this question: "You've often talked about how technology can empower people, how it can change their lives. Do you still have as much faith in technology today as you did when you started out 20 years ago?"[3]

As Jobs evolved as a leader, he demonstrated faith in people—specifically, his employees—in a period of unprecedented growth at Apple after his return.

"Faith," in this sense, is the building block of trust that fosters great teamwork, collaboration, and innovation. You can't possibly have one without the other. It's this building block of trust, in Jobs' case, that crystallized his relationships with his knowledge workers that helped launch the Apple products we can't live without today. Jobs believed that his employees were intelligent and capable, providing them with the necessary tools and resources to excel, while stepping aside to let them succeed and shine.

Leaders who adopt a "trust first" mindset, even before trust is earned, gain a significant advantage. By placing trust in people's abilities from the outset, they create an environment that encourages creativity and innovation, fostering a culture of trust and empowerment.

Assume Positive Intent

Whatever anybody says or does, assume positive intent. You will be amazed at how your whole approach to a person or problem becomes very different.

—Indra Nooyi

People are bound to make mistakes, sometimes repeatedly; this is practically guaranteed. But you know what Love in Action does? It extends trust first by assuming that people have good intentions behind their actions or words, even if they may seem questionable or challenging. It means giving them the benefit of the doubt and not immediately assuming the worst about them. This mindset can improve communication, relationships, and the work environment by building trust and understanding among team members.

One of the most diminishing factors impacting team performance is the absence of assuming positive intent in others. For example, when people interact with each other at work, you may see a team member or two interpreting the actions and words of others in a negative light without considering the possibility that their intentions may be good. This is inherent in human nature. Leaders do this, too. We hear something, and by the time we process our thoughts, we're going down a mental rabbit hole that later leads to misunderstandings and conflicts, which later results in inequities and biases that ultimately harm people and affect their performance.

Where does this come from? Various places. You can start with your family of origin. So many of us were conditioned to be cautious and distrustful of others. Whether it's being told "don't talk to strangers" as a child, false stereotypes of people reinforced into our thinking, or the current culture wars dividing us, we are suspicious of each other when we shouldn't be. People aren't inherently evil, and no human beings are born with hatred, intolerance, or suspicion. These are learned behaviors. Over time, we allow the worst of humanity to influence our thinking; we put up walls and get trapped into believing that people don't have our best interests at heart. Some may not, but they're in the minority. Then, these false beliefs, reinforced by media narratives in the nightly news, seep into our minds, and we take that to the workplace. The organization for which we work may hire someone who doesn't look, speak, or behave like us; we'll hear a still, small voice in our minds warning us to keep our guard up because we assume they may not be that trustworthy. The unwillingness to assume positive intent reinforces a two-way street: That particular employee may look at you, the person in charge, the same way and think, "My manager doesn't trust me," and proceed to walk on eggshells. While a "Spidey-sense" intuition may be understandable sometimes if an employee is guilty of repeated offenses, it can harm our work relationships if our default mode is to assume that people have negative intentions. Even worse is treating them as if we expect them to do something wrong.

The Place and Time for Assuming Positive Intent

We often get annoyed when someone doesn't do what we expect, especially if it keeps happening. If we don't curtail our impulses, we may be guilty of jumping to the wrong conclusions even without complete or accurate information about individual circumstances. This is the perfect place to assume positive intent, replace judgment with curiosity, and elevate listening to understand rather than condemn.

Indra Nooyi, former CEO of PepsiCo, says that her father's best advice was always to assume positive intent. "My father was an absolutely wonderful human being. From him I learned to always assume positive intent. Whatever anybody says or does, assume positive intent," Nooyi shares. "You will be amazed at how your whole approach to a person or problem becomes very different. When you assume negative intent, you're angry. If you take away that anger and assume positive intent, you will be amazed. Your emotional quotient goes up because you are no longer almost random in your response. You don't get defensive. You don't scream. You are trying to understand and listen because at your basic core you are saying, 'Maybe they are saying something to me that I'm not hearing.' So assume positive intent has been a huge piece of advice for me."[4]

Assuming positive intent means understanding the intentions behind people's angry words. Often, people are confused, hurt, or do not comprehend what is being asked of them. You can use techniques such as maintaining firm eye contact, asking questions from a place of trust, showing curiosity, and actively listening to understand different viewpoints.

Still, assuming positive intent is counterintuitive, which is even more reason to believe that people's actions are driven by good intentions. This shift of mindset fosters trust and mutual respect, where people feel comfortable communicating openly and honestly and where conflicts can be resolved more quickly.

Sally Helgesen, a global thought leader, author, and the foremost expert on the advancement of women's leadership, writes that, like any relationship, be it a marriage or any other kind, people must make compromises and adjustments. We need to respect ideas that we may not necessarily agree with and try to understand people who are different from ourselves. When I think about it, this may happen daily in the workplace!

One effective way to start assuming positive intent is by giving others the benefit of our goodwill, as suggested by Helgesen in her book *Rising Together*. This doesn't mean giving them the benefit of the doubt, which assumes negativity. We assume positive intent to extend our goodwill even when we're unsure if the other person deserves it. According to Helgesen, adopting this approach has several advantages. It helps us avoid negative or judgmental thinking that can weigh us down and make us overly critical. It enables us to build relationships with people who may seem different. It also expands our network of allies, enriches our connections, and allows us to embrace change. Ultimately, it helps us become bigger and better people.[5]

Revise Your Script

Helgesen suggests that to extend the benefit of our goodwill, we must change the negative scripts that impact our emotions when we encounter behaviors that make us uneasy. For instance, instead of assuming that Misty, the finance director, is showing off her opinions at the meeting or that Joe, the social media manager, appears shy and insecure and not someone you want to associate with, or that Mike, the new boss, reminds you of a previous toxic boss, therefore, he must be a jerk, we must question these assumptions and tell ourselves a new narrative, even if we don't fully believe it. For example, in each aforementioned case:

- "Misty is very articulate, and I could learn from her."
- "Joe might be reserved because he is new to the job."
- "Some of my co-workers from other departments have a high opinion of Mike—I need to learn why."

Extending our goodwill toward those we work with is a simple practice. However, despite its simplicity, Helgesen agrees that it's not so easy to implement. It demands that we exercise our emotional intelligence to pause our usual responses and create new ones. This approach enables us to display Love in Action.

Ultimately, assuming positive intent, rewriting our mental script, and extending the benefit of our goodwill will make workplaces freer and psychologically safer.

Lead Selflessly

Avoid putting yourself before others and you can become a leader among men.

—Lao Tzu

In Paul's teachings to the Corinthians on genuine love, he emphasized that love "does not seek its own."[*] This point is perhaps the cornerstone of his message. It's a typical inclination of human nature to insist on having things our way. Yet, this self-centeredness directly contrasts the tenets of Love in Action. Leading with agape love isn't focused on fulfilling its own desires but on caring for the needs and interests of others.

Consider the Corinthian community to which he wrote, which I've touched on in the introduction of this book. The Christians in Corinth exhibited extreme selfishness, demonstrated by their unwillingness to share during communal meals, eagerness to take legal action against fellow believers, and desire to hoard what they perceived as the "best" spiritual gifts for themselves. Instead of utilizing their gifts to benefit the community, they sought personal gain from them.

Fast-forward to current times, and the manner in which we live and work increasingly champions self-reliance and individualism; it's easy to fall into the trap of self-centeredness without realizing it. Self-centeredness can grow into a dangerous mindset that affects our relationships with others, as it did in Corinth. When we become overly focused on our own needs, desires, and perspectives, we risk alienating those around us, hindering collaboration, and stunting our ability to empathize with others. The way to push back against individual behaviors and systems that are greedy and self-serving to the detriment of others is simple: put others before self. Leadership in any setting or industry is best modeled by serving others instead of being served.

---

[*]1 Corinthians 13:4-5 (NASB).

Striking the Right Balance

Many people worry that being selfless and focused on others can cause them to overextend themselves and crash and burn. Worse, others with manipulative behaviors will see their generous giving nature as "open season" to make repeated requests at their expense. Are selfless people altruistically dysfunctional doormats? Let's set the record straight.

In his book *Give and Take*, Wharton professor Adam Grant explores why some individuals climb to the top of the success ladder while others plummet. In professional interactions, people typically fall into three categories: takers, matchers, or givers. Takers aim to extract as much as they can from others, matchers strive for an even exchange, and givers are the rare breed who contribute without expecting anything in return.

When examining the balance between self-interest and "other-interest" (selflessness), takers prioritize their own gain over others. In contrast, givers prioritize helping others, though sometimes to their detriment.

Grant found that selfless givers may dedicate their time and energy to others without considering their own needs, often at a cost. The right balance? Grant's research reveals that the most successful individuals usually possess both self-interest and concern for others simultaneously. Grant advocates for an approach he terms "otherish," where individuals prioritize benefiting others while pursuing their ambitions. There's no doormat or dumping ground for takers to take advantage of selfless givers because boundaries are set by striking a healthy balance. When givers blend concern for others with a healthy regard for themselves, they are less susceptible to burnout and more likely to flourish in both their personal and professional lives.

When leadership selflessly runs on all cylinders and emphasizes putting others first to accomplish mutual goals and fulfill visions together, it will release discretionary effort across the enterprise. It's a type of leadership that gives others credit and shines the spotlight on them, is quick to forgive, and delights in the growth and ambition of others.

Giving Credit to Others

Here's a scenario that may look familiar. The product development team designs a wonderful new app. The client is overjoyed about rolling it out, and the PR team is building the campaign for its launch.

And then this happens: The manager or executive in charge of the project steals the spotlight and takes all the credit for the work. No praise for the team, no celebration of everyone's success, no recognition of team members' contributions. When that happens, you can be almost certain that team morale will plummet to new depths.

This behavior has frequently been identified in research as a "bad boss" trait that leads to employee disengagement and even turnover. A 2019 BambooHR study found that "taking credit for employees' work" was rated the worst manager behavior by 63 percent of respondents and something they would consider worth quitting over.[6]

To be sure, one must ask: Could "taking credit for employees' work" actually work as a management strategy to get ahead? Or does it impede the manager and set him or her back? According to a study published on Forbes, which evaluated 3,800 leaders and measured their effectiveness when taking credit from others, "those leaders were rated as very ineffective leaders (13th percentile), while those who tried hard to give the credit to others were rated as some of the most effective leaders (85th percentile)."[7]

In my coaching work, I believe this toxic tendency of hogging the spotlight and taking all the credit is about individual performance. Managers with this attitude are playing for the name on the back of the jersey and are only concerned about their accomplishments and how they look to superiors.

Selfless leaders understand that they don't need the glory; they know what they've achieved. They don't seek validation because true validation comes from within. They stand back and celebrate their accomplishments by letting others shine, which helps boost others' confidence.

In 2007, Popeyes Louisiana Kitchen, the global chain of fried chicken fast-food restaurants, was in deep trouble. Profit was stagnant, and the company stock price had taken a nosedive to $13.00. The brand suffered, and franchise owners were butting heads with corporate.

Enter Cheryl Bachelder, who took the reins as CEO in what became one of the most high-profile turnaround stories ever documented. During her nine-year tenure as chief executive, Popeyes posted an average global sales growth of 8.4 percent and an average earnings per share growth of 14.1 percent between 2008 and 2015.[8] The franchisees were so geeked up with the turnaround that they began reinvesting in the brand, many of them remodeling their restaurants and building new ones around the world.

Bachelder was recognized as one of the restaurant industry's top executives not only for the remarkable 180° her company achieved but also for what the world is recognizing as a leadership philosophy founded on servant leadership.

In her 2015 book *Dare to Serve*, Bachelder outlines her philosophy for transforming Popeyes: to combine determination to succeed in business with personal humility to serve others.

This meant having a selfless dedication to serving the people who own the restaurants that serve the customers who walk in the door to experience scrumptious Louisiana cuisine.

This idea of customers coming second is not a new concept. More people-oriented companies are tuning in to the incredible financial return that comes after they invest first in the development and care of those on the front lines who serve their customers.

The "Spotlight" Problem

Bachelder uses a great illustration with powerful imagery to pinpoint the leadership problem solved by being a selfless servant leader. She writes that leadership is not unlike being on a Broadway stage. When we go to a Broadway show, the spotlight hits the stage, and we wait for the leading actor to come out and join us because we know that will be the beginning of the story.

Leadership, she notes, is much the same. When you get promoted to a leadership role, people wait to see who you are, how you're going to act, and how you're going to lead, and they form their conclusions from there.

Bachelder and her executive team concluded that too many leaders hunger for the spotlight, too many leaders want to stay in the spotlight, and too many leaders forget to shine the spotlight on others. "We have been taught the wrong rules of leadership," Bachelder said. "Those rules have been holding back the performance of the companies we lead."[9]

Her team collectively asked, "What if we turned the spotlight to the people we serve instead of keeping it to ourselves? And what would that look like?"

She created a culture with servant leadership principles to deliver superior performance and solve the spotlight problem. Bachelder held 60- to 90-minute coaching sessions with her leaders three times per month to find out where they were with their leadership and to talk about where they wanted to go next. She said that these coaching sessions were essential to nurture, love, and develop the capabilities of her leaders. She also acknowledges that a core selfless principle for how they conducted business—humility—is extremely hard to do. "We value it because if we said we were humble, we'd be lying on a daily basis," said Bachelder.[10]

Bachelder went on to advise leaders to remember the statement, "It's not about me," because once you let it become about you, people catch on to the idea that your position is to exercise power over them, and your decisions are seen as self-serving, rather than in service to others.

That's when we lose the focus of servant leadership and perhaps some of our team members in the process. Being a selfless leader must be great enough to be without pride, meaning that the *team* gets the credit.

Selfless Leadership Does Not Dwell on Mistakes

Holding onto a list of people's past grievances or keeping a record of their wrongdoing can be one of the most self-defeating behaviors a leader can adopt. Rather than dwelling on mistakes or grudges, effective leadership requires moving forward. If you find yourself keeping track of every misstep and error for things such as annual performance reviews, it's time to rethink that strategy. Address issues as they arise by having open, honest conversations immediately. If similar issues persist, it's important to engage more deeply with your team members. Check in with them personally; perhaps they are facing difficulties outside of work, or there's an underlying reason why the mistake continues to occur. Always start from a place of positive intent. If these recurring issues start to impact their job security, address the elephant in the room directly and clearly.

In the Corinthians account, Paul advised that "love does not take into account a wrong suffered."[†] Interestingly, the phrase "take into account" originates from the Greek word *logizomai*, which is a book-keeping term used to mean calculate or reckon, much like making an entry in a ledger.[11] Any good accountant will tell you that such entries are meant to create a permanent record for future reference. This practice is essential in business, but when it comes to leadership and dealing with people, this practice is not only unnecessary—it can actually be harmful.

You know what's more important? Forgiving the wrongs and giving people a second and even a third chance. Richard Sheridan, CEO of Menlo Innovations, has never had a policy of keeping a record of wrongs. "Some employees who have left us we wouldn't necessarily want back, but we'd still give even them a second chance. Maybe they've changed. Maybe we've changed," writes Sheridan.[12]

According to Sheridan, one employee at Menlo left the company three times, and felt compelled to return to Menlo each time when things didn't work out elsewhere. Some people would object and say this person is an unreliable job-hopper looking for the greener grass. Sheridan saw it differently. Every time this well-traveled employee returned, he came back a better person and became one of Menlo's most revered leaders. Rather than closing the door completely and keeping a permanent record of wrongs or holding on to a grudge that he left them in the first place, Sheridan welcomed his employee back with open arms each time, like a Prodigal Son. Sheridan wrote that, without this perspective, "we would not have benefited from having a smarter, gentler, more giving leader with us at those points in our journey and his."

---

†Ibid.

Remember, but Still Forgive

> *An eye for an eye for an eye for an eye ... ends in making*
> *everyone blind.*
>
> —Mahatma Gandhi

Forgiveness is rarely, if ever, discussed or practiced as part of workplace effectiveness. But it should be. Before you deem it some sort of religious fluff, practicing forgiveness in the workplace has a positive impact.

Journalist Megan Feldman Bettencourt knows a thing or two about the topic of forgiveness. In her book *Triumph of the Heart: Forgiveness in an Unforgiving World*, she explores how forgiveness, when practiced in the right ways, can lead to a better world.

As she puts it, "What has been traditionally seen as a religious ideal is now an important skill for anyone, whether atheist, agnostic, or believer, who seeks to live a healthy, happy life."[13]

Bettencourt explained how practicing forgiveness sparked dialogue and interest in the scientific community. In 1998, the research literature contained 58 empirical studies on forgiveness. By 2005, over 1,100 articles had been published.

Bettencourt mentions the important work by Dr. Frederic Luskin, the cofounder of the Stanford Forgiveness Project. Dr. Luskin defines forgiveness from the scientific perspective, calling it "an assertive creation of peace in the present." He concluded in multiple studies that forgiveness "elevates mood and increases optimism, while not forgiving is positively correlated with depression, anxiety, and hostility."

Dr. Luskin explains that blaming others for how we feel, rather than holding them accountable for their actions, traps us in victimhood and inaction. For example, it's more productive to report someone to HR for harmful, toxic behavior than to stew in resentment about it. He encourages people to "find the impersonal in the hurt" by recognizing that many others have likely faced similar hurts or disappointments, which are common and often not intended to cause personal harm. For instance, if a colleague at work yelled at you, it was probably not with the intention of hurting you deeply but because he or she was stressed or scared. Dr. Luskin acknowledges that offenses can have a personal impact, but understanding these perspectives with greater self-awareness can help reduce the pain and blame associated with them.

In *Triumph of the Heart*, Dr. Luskin says,

> When you don't forgive, you release all the chemicals of the stress response. Each time you react, adrenaline, cortisol, and norepinephrine enter the body. When it's a chronic grudge, you could think about it twenty times a day, and those chemicals limit creativity, they limit problem-solving. Cortisol and norepinephrine cause your brain to enter what we call 'the no-thinking zone,' and over time, they lead you to feel helpless and like a victim. When you forgive, you wipe all of that clean.

Translation: Not forgiving dumbs you down fast!

Making Forgiveness Work at Work

Interpersonal conflicts at work are par for the course. But they can leave lingering stress that clouds our ability to think clearly and empathize, making forgiveness seem out of reach. Based on their findings, the researchers provide suggestions for individuals and organizations to promote forgiveness in the workplace:

- **Lead by example**: Especially if you're in a leadership role, demonstrating forgiveness sets the tone for others. Leaders wield significant influence over organizational culture, so showing forgiveness regularly can inspire similar behavior in others.
- **Apologize and take steps to make amends**: Ignoring or deflecting responsibility can exacerbate distrust, often making the situation worse. Acknowledge mistakes and apologize quickly to promote forgiveness.

- **Create positive experiences together**: Rebuild trust by collaborating on shared tasks and engaging in activities that foster teamwork and cooperation.
- **Invest in training**: Teach, coach, or train practical forgiveness strategies to foster a more forgiving workplace culture.
- **Seek outside help, if necessary**: In some cases, involving neutral third parties can address conflicts, facilitate forgiveness, and promote reconciliation.

Remember the old saying, "Resentment is like taking poison and waiting for the other person to die." When you carry resentment, it doesn't just affect you; it seeps into your interactions with colleagues, poisoning the atmosphere.

I believe that a significant cause of both mental and physical illness in our workplaces today stems from an excessive focus on individual rights, which often comes at the expense of compassion and empathy. When everyone is solely concerned with their own interests, true success and happiness remain elusive. This mindset leads to a cycle where everyone takes, and nobody gives, resulting in a loss for all—even for those who may initially get what they want. Ultimately, a lack of love costs more than its benefits.

We often feel anger or envy when someone else receives a privilege or recognition we believe we deserve. This sense of entitlement stems from a focus on self rather than on our responsibilities or the needs of others, revealing a deeper lack of love. A truly effective leader prioritizes their duties and the support of others over their own perceived rights. This type of leadership is rooted in love—love that shifts focus from self-interest to the welfare of others, which is the ultimate remedy for self-centeredness.

Speak Your Truth

Vulnerability sounds like truth and feels like courage. Truth and courage aren't always comfortable, but they're never weakness.

—Brené Brown

In 1 Corinthians 13:6, Paul wrote that love "rejoices in the truth." The word "rejoices" comes from the Greek word "chairo," which means to be overjoyed or elated.[‡] Thus, the verse could be translated as "Love is overjoyed by the truth."

Corporate environments where people sweep the truth under the rug or withhold information are places stripped of joy. It breeds mistrust and skepticism. When people at work don't trust each other, they often won't share information or work together well. They might keep important details to themselves or not give their all because they're worried that someone will steal or misuse their ideas. Employees who feel distrustful spend more time worrying about protecting themselves than focusing on their work. This takes away from getting things done, which can slow down projects and decrease overall efficiency.

I have facilitated tense client meetings where getting at the truth— the raw nerve most people don't want to hit—was critical to cutting through unnecessary drama that disrupted teamwork. Unearthing the truth in a corporate setting can prove to be a formidable challenge, particularly when it comes to dealing with individuals.

I was hired by a leading residential treatment facility to assess the disconnect between managers and their VP. Eleven managers, most of whom were new to their roles, were experiencing challenges working together, which affected their client population. Additionally, many new managers needed help finding their place and voice as leaders within the organization.

When I was brought in to cut through the noise echoing between management layers, it took some effort to nudge people toward the truth. Once safety was established, hard conversations and radical

---

[‡]G5463—chairō—Strong's Greek Lexicon (kjv). Retrieved from www.blueletterbible.org/lexicon/g5463/kjv/tr/0-1/.

candor trickled in. Even when we arrived there, it was still surprising to a few senior managers who didn't expect the truth to be about them.

In one meeting, after I set clear ground rules for open discussion, we went around the table, and I asked each manager to share what blocks they were experiencing, with the VP listening at the head of the table. The usual and expected platitudes and formalities were exchanged; some managers complimented the VP's guidance in pushing an important treatment program forward, and the VP used his executive presence to acknowledge a team effort.

Then it happened. A female manager, identified as a "high potential" leader for advancement, spoke up, looking toward Ted (not his real name), her VP. "I love my job but am increasingly frustrated by your lack of support." After a few seconds of tense silence and a couple of raised eyebrows, she continued. "We work our tails off to ensure our clients are taken care of during their stay here, and I see the executive team committed to building up the program. I just wish I saw the same commitment to caring for our needs and building us up as managers."

A few heads looked down in an attempt to evade the conversation, but the truth was delivered. Other managers shared this sentiment, but only one person dared to express it. It was Ted's turn to speak: "I am a bit surprised by what I'm hearing, but I take responsibility for it. What should I be aware of to support you better as your leader?"

In hindsight, I have to acknowledge that Ted's humble response broke the ice. During the rest of the meeting, the managers and Ted engaged in a synergetic dialogue about several ways managers felt they could be supported, with Ted acknowledging their voices and agreeing to several action items for follow-through. I proceeded to coach Ted on the principles of servant leadership to address these gaps. After six months, the team began working together effectively. Their meetings became productive, and they learned to communicate transparently and collaboratively, even when they didn't always agree on strategies, but they learned to speak their truth on the matter. Truth quickly became an organizational value that commanded respect, loyalty, and commitment from all stakeholders. It also sped up the decision-making process.

LeadershipToolbox

Six Rules Toward Speaking Truth
Rule #1: Don't shoot the messenger. To arrive at the truth, every team member's opinion is important to uncover the larger group's or organization's truth. But beware: Things can go south quickly and tempers will flare when people take things personally and attack others for being honest. Boundaries for truth-telling must be set in place to ensure psychological safety.
Rule #2: Allow healthy disagreements to take place. If we want our teams to get at the truth, focusing on healthy disagreement, not hurtful feelings, is needed to arrive at the best possible solution.
Rule #3: Recognize that everyone views truth differently. Team members have unique experiences shaped by past setbacks and future hopes. Don't take for granted that others see truth the way you do. Make it a point to bring these perspectives into the open and discuss them.
Rule #4: Call on people who have not spoken up. Everyone should have a chance to share their thoughts before moving on, especially when the topic is controversial. You need the truth from every person to see the complete picture.
Rule #5: Set the expectation for team loyalty. If a team member's opinion is challenged and voted down, leaders need to be firm that no grudges are held or resentments allowed to fester, which could escalate to hard-to-manage toxicity. This is where humility comes in handy; team members need to accept and support the team's decision and move on.
Rule #6: Leaders speak last. When issues are put on the table, leaders must speak last so that they don't influence the thinking of their team. Most people have a hard time expressing a strong opinion that's different than the leader's opinions. If you have various levels of experience or tenure in the room, make sure that those who are junior to you go first.

If we're going to show Love in Action, everyone on the team must feel heard and valued. Let's face it: Conversations can get rushed and emotional during tough times. People might start to blame each other, and frustration can build up. Others will clam up and shut down. This can lead to hasty decisions that make team members feel their opinions don't matter. Remember that most people quit their jobs because they don't feel appreciated and heard by their bosses.

Truthful decision making is essential for the future of any team or organization. Finding the truth takes time, discipline, and effort but encourages maximum participation and leads to the best outcomes. Truthful leaders always prioritize these qualities through love and care.

Truthfulness Demands Radical Transparency

Bridgewater Associates is one of the world's largest investment management firms that values transparency. To maintain open communication and avoid misunderstandings, the company records every meeting and makes the recordings available to all employees. This policy serves several purposes, including as a learning tool, a way to promote precision, and reduce politics in decision making.

The Founder of Bridgewater, Ray Dalio, has said, "My most important principle is that getting at the truth is essential for getting better." He says, "We get at truth through radical transparency and putting aside our ego barriers in order to explore our mistakes and personal weaknesses so that we can improve."[14]

One of the most celebrated cases of transparency was the turnaround of Intel, the world's biggest chipmaker that is in just about every computer on the planet. When their former CEO, Bob Swan, took over the helm in 2019, Intel's culture was a hot mess. They were a typical bureaucratic company with outdated corporate practices. Swan told *The New York Times* that Intel had "a hidden problem" and its 110,000 employees "needed to confront issues more openly." So, he exposed it in plain view of everyone by unifying his global team to become transparent. Swan told his employees, "If you have a problem, put it on the table." He urged his employees to be "bolder, be more attentive to customers, and honor truth and transparency."[15] Intel did not foster a culture of intellectual or emotional honesty at the time, so he changed that. Slowly, this practice trickled down to lower ranks. Swan said the managers he inherited saw the hoarding of information as a good thing. Interestingly enough, hoarding information from others, in fact, is one of the most effective ways to kill trust, not promote trust.

To counter the effects of hoarding, one Intel executive pushed for more inclusive ways to design products. He enlisted teams from different groups around the company to share information and pitch in their ideas, which broke the rules of the previous culture.

Intel used to live by bureaucracy like most organizations today. Now, Intel managers are told to cut down on meetings, and they encourage their employees to begin presentations by listing problems first, which gets to the root of issues and solutions faster. This has created a more agile organization with everyone moving in the same direction.

Intel also dealt with heavy bureaucracy by fostering intrapreneurship—encouraging employees to think and act like individual entrepreneurs and empowering them to take action, embrace risk, and make decisions on their own.

As a result, Intel has sped up product design by allowing input from multiple groups, something you never saw prior to Swan. Collaboration between manufacturing and design engineers, which had been estranged in the past, also improved.

To summarize all these illustrations and strategies we have uncovered into a succinct statement, here's the why of transparency, the bottom line: Being transparent will address the "hidden problems" in your own organization. When leaders are more transparent, employees can better understand why certain decisions are made. It promotes inclusion, idea sharing, and psychological safety among teams so that when problems arise, employees can confront issues more openly, be more honest with one another, and collaborate more effectively.

Truthfulness Demands Tough Love

Situations call for speaking the truth with tough love—for example, when confronting and maybe even terminating someone for underperforming. Yes, I did mention in Chapter 6 how the co-CEOs of Next Jump Associates have a "never fire anyone" rule. But let's face it: At times, we need to courageously speak our truth about an employee, colleague, or co-worker so we can steer them in the direction they need to go, whether inside or outside our corporate walls.

Chuck Runyon, cofounder and CEO of the international mega-fitness chain Anytime Fitness (more than 4,700 locations), encourages emotional expression in the workplace and has fostered a culture where employees can be human. He also co-wrote the book *Love Work* with his cofounder Dave Mortensen, where they document their leadership principles to build a high-engagement, high-performance, Love in Action culture.

I asked Runyon about one of his biggest leadership mistakes and what he learned. He said,

> We've made the mistake of keeping a loyal, hard-working person too long. We loved them and their past work, but they were no longer suited for what the role required. We learned that even the most popular employees have limitations. And the longer you delay making hard decisions, the harder they become.[16]

Many leaders fear getting too close to employees because they fear that emotions will cloud their judgment when making hard decisions for the business. Runyon told me they've experienced this firsthand at Anytime Fitness when having to replace loyal, hardworking employees with others who are better equipped to suit the needs of a growing company. "But love requires honesty and, while admittedly difficult to deliver, honesty is the purest form of tough love," said Runyon.[17]

Truthfulness Demands Emotional Honesty

You cannot speak your truth without emotional honesty and fearless vulnerability. This is uncharted territory, which is challenging for many of my management clients. I say "challenging" because these courageous skills, when mastered, work wonders in squashing ambiguity, setting boundaries, getting to the root of a problem, and diffusing conflict. Both are sought-after leadership competencies I'm often asked to help develop in managers. Why is this the case, you may wonder?

Many of us were raised to keep the emotional parts of ourselves closed off from others, and as a result, as we move into leadership roles, we often turn off our emotions. On top of that, we're told to check our feelings at the door, so we compartmentalize and pretend to act professionally.

When we keep our distance as managers and executives, we invite emotional disconnectedness. If you're emotionally disconnected from your team members, it will undermine your self-confidence as a leader. People will look at you and sense that you're not 100 percent authentic. And that can hold you back.

But let's get one thing straight: Getting to the core of emotional honesty isn't a license to offend and speak your mind without filters to intentionally hurt others. There's a term for that: a total jerk.

Emotionally honest people are respected because they hold themselves and others to a higher standard. They're also not doormats. When the rubber meets the road, their integrity will call you on the carpet for wrongdoing or injustice. They speak their mind and don't rely on cryptic hints or other passive-aggressive tactics to get their point across.

Emotional honesty means, perhaps, ending a relationship, firing an employee, or severing a partnership that no longer defines one's true nature. It is more the reason for one's likability.

The Power of Vulnerability

Dr. Brené Brown's now-historic TED Talk, "The Power of Vulnerability," stressed the critical role of leaders in connecting with and inspiring others. Some might say vulnerability is all too touchy-feely and inappropriate for business. Others may say they're just not wired for it—it's not in their personality makeup. Let me tell you why none of these things are true.

First, Brown explains that vulnerability is a state of uncertainty, relational risk, and emotional exposure. It is the emotion we feel when we put ourselves out there. We're often taught not to be vulnerable, even though we are taught to be brave.

According to Brown's research, courage cannot exist without vulnerability. She shared a story of her work with the Seattle Seahawks. During one session, she asked a group of players for an example of a courageous act that doesn't require vulnerability. They huddled for a minute and came back and said, "There is no courage without vulnerability, not on or off the field. If you're not all in, if you're not putting yourself out there, you just can't be brave."[18]

Brown believes that we tend to become more guarded because we lack trust and confidence at work. We put on a façade of who we think we are supposed to be at work. We "armor up" by using cynicism, perfectionism, and the need to be right instead of being open to learning and making mistakes. Sometimes, these forms of armor can be rewarded at work, which discourages people from being truly vulnerable.

Vulnerability is about trust—the backbone of successful leadership. Employees and leaders who trust one another learn to be comfortable being open with one another about their failures, weaknesses, and even fears. This is why vulnerability must be a fearless act and a strength of leaders who want to up their game.

Vulnerability-based trust is predicated on the simple—and practical idea—that people who aren't afraid to admit the truth are not going to engage in the kind of political drama that sucks away everyone's time and energy and, more importantly, gets in the way of accomplishing goals and results.

It's why vulnerability is so key in leading others. One of the biggest lessons any leader will learn is to be open and honest about disappointment, failure, or sadness—not to smooth it over, or in any way feel like you don't face it directly.

Take the Mask Off

Reaching this level of vulnerability-based trust is totally doable, but that doesn't mean it isn't hard. It's hard because it means letting go of the mask.

I'm talking about the masks we wear at one time or another that keep parts of us hidden, as Intel's Bob Swan explained earlier. Masks keep us from showing up as who we truly are, and that keeps us from speaking our truth.

In workplaces where people hide behind masks, you cannot fully risk being open with each other due to the lack of trust. Learning to display your best authentic self and remove the mask will help you to connect better with other people and build trust over time.

Wearing masks on different occasions in my younger life was a toxic habit before I eventually grew into a more emotionally honest person (trust me, I'm still a work in progress). In dating relationships that showed long-term promise, whenever discussion points came up around finances, religion, sex, and child-rearing, I downplayed the scene, let my ego dictate ("No worries, not an issue"), and allowed the moment to slip under my fake calm and calculated demeanor. The mask I wore led to manipulative behaviors, self-deception, and self-sabotage that ended in one terrifying lesson: chasing, conquering, marrying, and quickly divorcing my first wife after she saw through my act and uncovered the person behind the mask. After serious soul-searching, I finally broke the cycle and am now happily married (16 years and counting) to the first woman I ever showed 100 percent emotional honesty. I took the mask off.

The Upside

When you show up with fearless vulnerability and emotional honesty, you don't hesitate to do the right thing. You never have to second-guess yourself. Who you are, what you do, and what you believe in align perfectly. You have the strength and openness to deal with problems quickly instead of procrastinating, avoiding conflict, or sweeping things under the rug.

You are true to your character regardless of outside pressures or temptations to act otherwise. You are willing to accept the consequences of being true to what you consider to be right at the core of your being. You don't cave in to others who try to dictate your course. You take control of life and move forward with confidence.

You are consistent in who you are and what you do. You'll always put your best foot forward and treat every person and situation the same.

There's one promise I'll make as I end this chapter. You *will* experience all these benefits, but the shift only happens when you consciously choose to drop the masks and show up with your most authentic self. It will take work and courage, but like any change in behavior, practice, practice, and more practice is the only way to rewire the brain so that new habits can form. Your life will dramatically change in a powerful and positive direction. I've seen it in myself and my clients, and I know that I will see it in you, too.

To summarize, the foundation of being a trustworthy leader is built upon several key pillars that we have discussed. It involves confidence in others, believing in people, putting your hope in them, and remaining steadfast during challenging times. It's also a two-way street. Leaders who see others as trustworthy extend trust as an act of unconditional love. When someone makes a mistake, a trustworthy leader will choose the most favorable action and assume that someone is innocent until proven guilty.

This cycle of trustworthiness fosters freedom and autonomy; whenever there's doubt, a leader errs on the favorable side rather than throw someone under the bus because they believe the best in others. And since Love in Action is a harbor of trust, love's first response is to restore when that trust is broken. To that end, a leader's attitude toward an employee starts fresh following a mistake—a clean slate. That's why people in healthy cultures of high trust take risks and feel psychologically safe to exercise their creativity, take ownership of their work, "fail forward," learn together, communicate ideas openly, and provide input to decisions without reprimand—all because there's trust there.

Action Plan

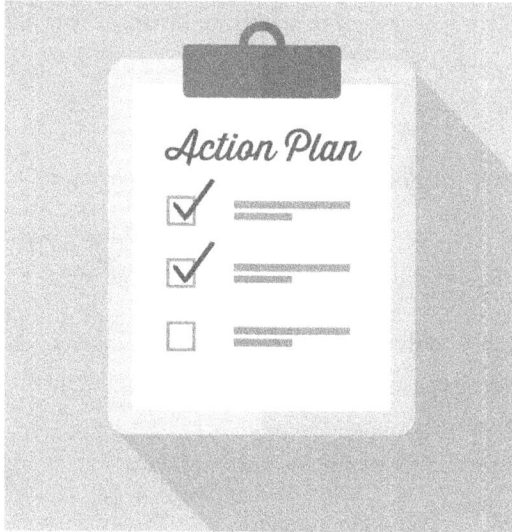

Action Items for Assume Positive Intent

1. First, recognize your automatic tendency to assume negative intentions when something goes wrong.
2. Next, consciously look for positive intent by giving people the benefit of the doubt.
3. Finally, be intentional about learning the details of the situation, getting curious, and making a fair assessment.

Action Items for Lead Selflessly

1. Practice removing obstacles that make it hard for employees to do their best work.
2. Ask your direct reports, "How can I help you?" or "What can I do—and *not* do—to help you be successful?"
3. Catch people doing things right—and show people you "see them."
4. Find opportunities to develop people's skills. Think about what would benefit those you serve by improving their skills.

5. Be more selfless with your time. Have one-on-one meetings not to benefit you as their manager but because they would benefit your employees first.

♀ Action Items for Speak Your Truth (Transparency)

Get together in a group of three to five employees, with you, the manager, acting as facilitator. The group's challenge is to:

- Assess how well the team/company embraces as opposed to battles transparency. Identify current practices that promote transparency and those that don't.
- Brainstorm how improvements can be made in strengthening transparency.
- Share ideas with other team(s) in the company.
- Come up with an agreed upon action plan for implementing key initiatives.

♀ Action Item for Speak Your Truth (Vulnerability)

Lead by example: Embrace vulnerability and share your uncertainties. You're doing it to show others that you are genuine and approachable— human and humane. To further build trust, foster psychological safety so that team members feel safe to take risks and be vulnerable in front of each other without reprimand or ridicule.

♀ Action Item for Speak Your Truth (Emotional Honesty)

Share personal stories and mistakes made: Personal stories will let your tribe know that you are human and imperfect, just like the rest of them. By sharing the mistakes you've made and the lessons you learned from them, people will no longer fear and hide when they make theirs. Storytelling lets your people know you've been in their shoes and helps you connect emotionally with them.

Conclusion

You can have everything you want in life if you just help enough people get what they want in life

—Zig Ziglar

It's been 20 years since I lay on my bathroom floor, writhing in pain from the cumulative effects of toxic stress catalyzed by a leader and a workplace that failed to embody the principles of Love in Action. I have since learned that exceptional leaders the world over operate differently. They have this natural tendency—something from deep within—to want to help and serve others and alleviate their suffering. As mentioned earlier in this book, people hesitate to bring their emotions to the workplace. Yet, Love in Action leaders unabashedly *rely* on their emotions to get to the root of problems; they have this ability to feel what others feel and do everything in their power to clear the path to people's growth and success. It is love demonstrated by the principles in this book that will lead to high organizational performance, innovation, customer retention, profitability, and less employee turnover. From this point in the story, we must evolve as leaders and managers. We cannot go back to how things were. We must face the hard reality that the future of leadership for generations to come is humane, and so much better when Love in Action is activated.

What No Longer Works

Many traditional management practices are outdated, stifling the human spirit and hindering Love in Action. As I bring us home, let's revisit some rather obsolete practices. Take, for instance, the tendency to hoard information, which only serves to disadvantage people by limiting transparency and hindering the flow of information.

The annual performance review often feels like a mere checkbox exercise, where overwhelmed managers hastily fulfill HR requirements and unload a barrage of feedback on employees all at once. This approach leaves employees feeling bewildered, inundated, and sometimes even frustrated.

Micromanagement remains prevalent, even in 2025. Managers often fail to value or trust their team members sufficiently to allow them the freedom to leverage their strengths, which were the very reasons they were hired. Consequently, employees find themselves suffocated by managers who make decisions unilaterally, without consulting the team. This breeds a culture of mistrust, stifling creativity and high performance among talented employees.

Bureaucracy, another relic of the industrial revolution, embodies control and a lack of trust. When it becomes unhealthy and extreme, it strangles productivity and work processes. You'll encounter too many layers of management approval, hindering progress and fostering a focus on micromanagement.

Consider whether your organization glorifies overwork. Many of us have experienced environments where clocking in 55 or 60 hours a week is seen as a badge of honor—a cultural expectation. Those who don't comply may face judgment, leading to guilt and conformity to the overwork culture. Sadly, our society often rewards those who sacrifice personal time for work and eventually crash and burn.

I've noticed a widespread issue of unclear communication among managers. As I highlighted in Chapter 2, one major factor contributing to stress and stress-related illnesses, such as heart disease, is the absence of clear and realistic goals and expectations set by leaders. Managers who lack clear communication will often change direction daily or weekly. So, employees have no idea what is really going on, and no one knows the *real* truth of the current situation or what the future holds. This causes confusion, fear, and anxiety in the minds of workers.

Just prioritizing profit margins is outdated and inhumane. Plenty of research confirms that when companies prioritize serving all stakeholders, with a special focus on their employees, financial outcomes actually improve. That's the heart of Love in Action: prioritize people, and they'll naturally prioritize customers. With that focus, the business thrives.

We've learned that a large percentage of managers use money as a carrot-and-stick method of incentivizing workers because they don't want to do the hard work of building relationships and connecting with their people. Money is important, but it's not sustainable if the work environment leaves people disengaged and disconnected from their leaders and their work. People must be intrinsically motivated, and money alone won't do that.

We also know that internal competition between co-workers is unhealthy. I have fired clients whose employees are expected to compete fiercely against each other. If you've experienced this as an employee, it's inhumane. Managers will enforce this tactic with unrealistic performance measures focusing on individual rather than team performance. This is simply not sustainable.

This list of the atrocities of current management practices is much longer, but I'll stop here. We have come to expect these things because most of us have experienced them in our careers, which is reinforced and passed on to others when they become managers.

If we continue to tread this path with those outdated management practices, you can bet that your employees' interactions with you as leaders and managers, their interactions with their colleagues, and especially your customers will come across in ways that don't work in your favor unless you choose a more humane path.

A Final Plea

We come full circle, bringing you back to what I emphasized in Chapter 1 about the importance of embracing a fresh mindset—a new way of thinking about how to view the role of leadership. Because the current model was never about creating value in human beings doing the work. It is broken.

The shift is obvious and clear. We've learned that caring for employees significantly enhances their work experience, boosting performance, engagement, loyalty, and commitment throughout the organization. When employees feel valued, they'll end their day with a smile and eager to return; they'll come home to their loved ones and say, "I love my job and can't wait to be back tomorrow."

I've been documenting evidence for this book for two decades. Actionable and practical love *can* and *will* raise the employee experience to new heights. I've shown you that this kind of actionable love has been proven to improve performance and lead to business outcomes. This is no longer a pie-in-the-sky theory. It's real. And it starts with you.

Many of my coaching clients have come to a crucial realization: as managers, their primary focus should be their people. It's quite an eye-opener! When I chat with newly promoted managers about their experience, I often hear, "I'm really thankful for this chance, but I'm swamped. I have people coming to me all day with issues to solve, and I just can't find the time to do my own work."

How do you think I respond? I tell them that the heart of what they do as their primary role as a leader is to support, guide, and energize their team. I say, "When you step into a leadership position, your priorities shift; leading, nurturing, and guiding your team to success becomes your key responsibility." It's the whole *why* of Love in Action. But it will never work if they don't have the right mindset and belief. "When you sign up for it," I tell them, "it has to be an expectation of your role and job description."

If you make this transformation, I'm here to tell you that it will change your leadership and life.

So, we arrive at our final stop in your Love in Action growth. Don't remove your seatbelts just yet. For some of you, the journey may be about to begin.

The Question Every Leader Needs to Ask

I will leave you with one prerequisite—something for you to reflect on and consider deep down in your heart. To seriously elevate your impact and influence as a leader, you must remember that leadership is about service and making those around you better. There's no way around it. This is how love manifests itself as a business value and transforms organizations.

To assess where you are against the high measure of an impactful, loving leader, there is one very powerful question you need to ask right now:

> What am I doing every day to improve lives and help people to flourish?

That's what it comes down to. A leader's ultimate goal is to act as a vehicle to help others achieve their goals and dreams—to be the catalyst that creates ripples in the lives of others, which will continue to spread and grow.

Love in Action ultimately involves influencing people for their growth and development, unleashing their potential to impact businesses and society positively. What leader doesn't want that?

When you can learn, adapt, and habitually apply the lessons in this book, remove obstacles in their path, set people up for success, and improve their lives and livelihoods, you will love them well. And when you showcase in true form the virtues and practices of Patience, Kindness, Humility, Advocacy, and Trustworthiness, you will never again be seen in the same light; your humane leadership will only get better from here.

I've given you what you need to get your Love in Action business strategy into motion. The question is, will you step up to the challenge and make it happen? Will you be that leader the world desperately needs in times of suffering, division, and distress? What are you committed to?

It's now your turn.

Appendix A

The Self-Awareness Outcomes Questionnaire (SAOQ)

The SAOQ is a self-report questionnaire designed to assess the frequency with which respondents experience outcomes related to the development of self-awareness. The SAOQ identifies the main impacts of self-awareness on people's day-to-day lives (including work-related outcomes) and can be used to measure the specific effects of self-awareness interventions or training programs.

You may use this questionnaire for free, provided you agree to these two conditions:

1. You will use the SAOQ for noncommercial educational or research purposes only. This means that no one is charging anyone a fee.
2. You agree to share some of your data (raw test-scores, age, gender, and (if available) occupation, as well as a brief explanation of the sample's size, language, and country) with the author of the scale, Dr. Anna Sutton (anna.sutton@waikato.ac.nz). Data will be used for the purpose of further validation.

For commercial use and licensing, please contact Dr. Anna Sutton directly (anna.sutton@waikato.ac.nz).

Instructions

Following is a list of statements about your general experiences. Using the scale, please indicate how frequently you experience or engage in each of them.

Never	Rarely	Occasionally	Frequently	Almost always	N/A
1	2	3	4	5	N/A

There is no "right" or "wrong" answer as everyone is different, so simply answer according to your own experience. (If you are not currently working, you may find that a few questions are not applicable to you. In this case, please choose the N/A response.)

	1	**2**	**3**	**4**	**5**	**N/A**
1	I learn about myself and how I see the world					
2	I understand my emotions					
3	I am content with my work situation					
4	I find it scary to try something new or step out of what I know					
5	I focus on ways of amending my behavior that would be useful					
6	I have fun					
7	I recognize the stress and worry in my current work					
8	I feel vulnerable					
9	I reassess my own and others' responsibilities					
10	I have compassion and acceptance for others					
11	I see my work life as something I have power to affect					
12	I feel my emotions deeply					
13	I'm aware of my abilities and limitations					
14	I am objective					
15	I understand how I work within a team					
16	I have had to revisit difficult past experiences					
17	I "observe" myself					
18	I understand myself well					
19	I can "take a step back" from situations to understand them better					
20	I feel exposed					
21	I feel generally positive about self-awareness					

	1	2	3	4	5	N/A
22	I am consistent in different situations or with different people					
23	I think about how my personality fits with my work role					
24	I find that making changes is difficult and scary					
25	I have insight into myself					
26	I stop and think before judging					
27	I have changed the way I work					
28	I feel guilty for criticizing others					
29	I look at why people act the way they do					
30	I am confident					
31	I take control of my work					
32	I am continuing to work on and develop myself					
33	I interact well with colleagues or peers					
34	I think about how as colleagues or peers we interact with each other					
35	I am realistic about myself					
36	I feel on the whole very comfortable with the way I am					
37	I am reflective					
38	I have a good self-image					

Descriptives and Norms

The SAOQ consists of 38 items measuring 4 subscales. In a UK sample (76% female, 77% in full-time work), the following means, SDs and Cronbach alpha reliabilities were obtained for each subscale:

Subscale	No. items	Mean	SD	α
Reflective self-development (RSD)	11	3.94	0.58	0.87
Acceptance (Acc)	11	3.85	0.52	0.83
Proactive at work (Pro)	9	3.74	0.68	0.81
Emotional costs	7	3.10	0.67	0.77

Scoring

To score the SAOQ, calculate the mean for each scale using the following key: (N/A responses should be left out of the calculation).

Higher scores represent a greater frequency of experienced outcomes.

Subscale	Mean of items
Reflective self-development (RSD)	1, 5, 9, 13, 17, 21, 25, 29, 32, 35, 37
Acceptance (Acc)	2, 6, 10, 14, 18, 22, 26, 30, 33, 36, 38
Proactive at work (Pro)	3, 7, 11, 15, 19, 23, 27, 31, 34
Emotional costs	4, 8, 12, 16, 20, 24, 28

Citing the SAOQ

Sutton, A. 2016. "Measuring the Effects of Self-Awareness: Construction of the Self- Awareness Outcomes Questionnaire." *Europe's Journal of Psychology* 12 (4) 645–58. doi: 10.5964/ejop.v12i4.1178.

Notes

Introduction

1. Lewis, Amini, and Lannon, *A General Theory of Love*.

Chapter 1

1. "Dozens of Former 'Ellen Show' Employees Say Executive Producers Engaged in Rampant Sexual Misconduct And Harassment," *BuzzFeed News*.
2. "Toxic Culture Is Driving the Great Resignation," *MIT Sloan Management Review*.
3. Ibid.
4. Ibid.
5. Nyberg et al., "Managerial Leadership and Ischaemic Heart Disease Among Employees: The Swedish WOLF Study," 51–55.
6. Ibid.
7. Lynch, "Why Your Workplace Might Be Killing You."
8. McGregor, "This Professor Says the Workplace Is the Fifth Leading Cause of Death in the U.S."
9. Ibid.
10. Walsh, "The Workplace Is Killing People and Nobody Cares."
11. Chapman and Sisodia, *Everybody Matters: The Extraordinary Power of Caring for Your People Like Family*, 9.
12. Friedman, "A Friedman Doctrine—The Social Responsibility of Business Is to Increase Its Profits."
13. Author, "Business Roundtable Redefines the Purpose of a Corporation to Promote 'An Economy That Serves All Americans.'"
14. Sipe, and Frick, *Seven Pillars of Servant Leadership: Practicing the Wisdom of Leading by Serving*.
15. Engelberg, "The Violence in Your Business Language Diminishes You and Your Company."
16. Beck, "Eufear: Embracing Our Fears' Positivity."

17. Marchwinski, "Rich Sheridan on How to Succeed by Building a Strong Learning Culture."
18. Ibid.

Chapter 2

1. "Whole Foods' John Mackey on Capitalism's Moral Code," *Harvard Business Review.*
2. Ornish, "Creating a High Trust Organization."
3. Lemoine, Hartnell, and Leroy, "Taking Stock of Moral Approaches to Leadership: An Integrative Review of Ethical, Authentic, and Servant Leadership," 148–187.
4. Schwantes, "This Best-Selling Leadership Expert Reveals the Simple Habits That Separate Successful People From Everyone Else."
5. Ostroff, Atwater, and Feinberg, "Understanding Self-Other Agreement: A Look at Rater and Ratee Characteristics, Context, and Outcomes," 333–375.
6. Sala, "Executive Blind Spots: Discrepancies Between Self-and Other-Ratings," 222.
7. Sutton, "Measuring the Effects of Self-Awareness: Construction of the Self-Awareness Outcomes Questionnaire," 645.
8. Brainy Quote, "The World's Largest Quotation Site."
9. Fitzgerald, *Barbara Walters Interviews General Norman Schwarzkopf (20/20).*
10. Encyclopedia.com., "Norman Schwarzkopf."
11. Crowley, "Why Engagement Happens in Employees' Hearts, Not Their Minds."
12. Ibid.
13. Fredrickson, *Love 2.0: Creating Happiness and Health in Moments of Connection.*
14. Crowley, "Why Engagement Happens in Employees' Hearts, Not Their Minds."
15. Ibid.

Chapter 3

1. Schwantes, *Love in Action podcast.*
2. Sluss, "Becoming a More Patient Leader."
3. Schwantes, *Love in Action podcast.*

4. Ibid.

5. Shanker, "Self-Regulation vs. Self-Control."

6. Comer and Sekerka, "Taking Time for Patience in Organizations," 16–23.

7. Ibid.

8. Schwantes, "7 Strategies to Master Your Workplace Anger."

9. Goleman, "Self-Regulation: A Star Leader's Secret Weapon."

10. Pearson and Porath, "On the Nature, Consequences and Remedies of Workplace Incivility: No Time for 'Nice'? Think Twice," 7–18.

11. Reason, "Expanding the Conversation: Perspective Taking as a Civic Outcome of College."

12. Grant and Berry, "The Necessity of Others Is the Mother of Invention: Intrinsic and Prosocial Motivations, Perspective Taking, and Creativity," 73–96.

13. Sluss, "Becoming a More Patient Leader."

14. Ibid.

15. Schnitker and Emmons, *Research in the Social Scientific Study of Religion*, 177–207.

16. Comparably, "Study: The Worst Traits in a Boss."

17. Dunlop, *Hey Bosses: Here's What Gen Z Actually Wants at Work*.

18. Ibid.

19. Pankowski, *Personal Communication*.

20. Dale, "Audio-Visual Methods in Teaching."

21. Ibid.

22. DeSteno et al., "Gratitude: AR Tool for Reducing Economic Impatience," 1262–1267.

23. Seppälä, "Breathing-Based Meditation Decreases Posttraumatic Stress Disorder Symptoms in US Military Veterans: A Randomized Controlled Longitudinal Study,"... 397–405.

24. Badaracco, *Step Back: Bringing the Art of Reflection Into Your Busy Life*.

Chapter 4

1. Luscombe, "At Least 80 People Form Human Chain to Rescue Stranded Group in Gulf of Mexico."

2. Haidt, *Flourishing: Positive Psychology and the Life Well-Lived*.

3. Ibid.

4. Vianello, et al., "Elevation at Work: The Effects of Leaders' Moral Excellence," 390–411.

5. Dunlop et al., *Hey Bosses: Here's What Gen Z Actually Wants at Work.*

6. Brown, "The Power of Vulnerability."

7. Ibid.

8. Zaki, "How to Sustain Your Empathy in Difficult Times."

9. Harter, "Percent Who Feel Employer Cares About Their Wellbeing Plummets."

10. Sinar et al., "High-Resolution Leadership: A Synthesis of 15,000 Assessments Into How Leaders Shape the Business Landscape."

11. Ibid.

12. Zaki, *The war for kindness: Building empathy in a fractured world.*

13. Ibid.

14. Cava, "Microsoft's Satya Nadella is counting on culture shock to drive growth."

15. Zaki, "How to Sustain Your Empathy in Difficult Times."

16. Ibid.

17. Weiner, "Managing Compassionately."

18. Weiner, "Big misconception about managing compassionately is that it's a 'soft' skill."

19. Dutton, Quinn, and Pasick, *The Heart of Reuters.*

20. Ibid.

21. Ibid.

22. Barsade, "What's Love Got to Do With It?"

23. Barsade and O'Neill, "What's Love Got to Do With It? A Longitudinal Study of the Culture of Companionate Love and Employee and Client Outcomes in the Long-Term Care Setting," 551–598.

24. Ibid.

Chapter 5

1. Wright et al., "The Psychological Significance of Humility," 3–12.

2. Porter et al., " Clarifying the Content of Intellectual Humility: A Systematic Review and Integrative Framework," 573–585.

3. Deffler, Leary, and Hoyle, "Knowing What You Know," 255–259.

4. Gerut, *Small-Cap Institute Presents* Podcast.

5. Gino, "The Business Case for Curiosity," 48–57.

6. Fourmy, "Why Executives Need to Practice Vulnerable Leadership—and How to Do It."

7. The Silicon Valley Historical Association, *Steve Jobs on Failure* [video].

8. Grant, How to Get the Help You Need, 142–145.

9. Flynn, and Lake, "If You Need Help, Just Ask," 128–143.

10. Brooks and Gino, "Asking Advice Makes a Good Impression," 26–27.

11. Kets de Vries, "Why It's So Hard to Ask for Help."

12. Ibid.

13. Geller, and Bamberger, "The Impact of Help Seeking on Individual Task Performance," 487–497.

14. Schaubroeck, and Fink, "Facilitating and Inhibiting Effects of Job Control and Social Support on Stress Outcomes and Role Behavior," 167–195.

15. Ancona, Bresman, and Kaeufer, "The Comparative Advantage of X-teams."

16. Lucas, "Costco Employees Just Voted to Unionize. The Company's Response Is Remarkable."

17. Ibid.

18. Thorbecke, "Zoom Will Lay Off 1,300 Employees and CEO Is Taking a Massive Pay Cut."

19. Ibid.

20. LEADx, "Richard Branson's 7 Secrets to Leadership."

21. Seppala, "What Bosses Gain by Being Vulnerable," 2–5.

22. Gino, "Why Curiosity Matters," 47–61.

23. Ibid.

24. The Coach, Reverse mentoring [Video].

25. Kashdan et al., "When Curiosity Breeds Intimacy," 1369–1402.

26. Gino, "Why Curiosity Matters."

27. Ibid.

28. Kashdan et al., "Curiosity Protects Against Interpersonal Aggression," 87–102.

29. Bryant, "I've Interviewed Hundreds of CEOs. They All Share This One Habit of Mind."

30. Cunningham, "Trying to Change the World Bank."

31. Schwantes, "Are Women Better Leaders, With Tomas Chamorro-Premuzic."

32. Ibid.

33. Coyle, The Culture Playbook: 60 Highly Effective Actions to Help Your Group Succeed, 103.

Chapter 6

1. Ibid.

2. Gartner. "Future of Work Reinvented."

3. Sheridan, Chief Joy Officer.

4. Durose, Cooper, and Snyder, *Recidivism of Prisoners Released in 30 States in 2005.*

5. Shuit, "Delancey Street Rehab Center to Open in L.A."

6. Marr et al., "Do I Want to Know?" 285–297.

7. US Department of Health and Human Services, "New Surgeon General Advisory Raises Alarm About the Devastating Impact of the Epidemic of Loneliness and Isolation in the United States."

8. Schawbel, *Back to Human.*

9. Loneliness and the Workplace, *Cigna.*

10. Harvard University, "Loneliness in America."

11. Chancellor et al., "Everyday Prosociality in the Workplace, 507–517.

12. Ibid, 511.

13. Chen, "Remote Workers Are Losing Out on Promotions, New Data Shows."

14. Ibid.

15. History.com, "Ford Factory Workers Get 40-hour Week."

16. Lynch, "Why Your Workplace Might Be Killing You."

17. Weller, "Forget the 9 to 5—Research Suggests There's a Case for the 3-Hour Workday."

18. Hansen, *Great at Work.*

19. Lau and Sigurdardottir, "The Shorter Work Week Really Worked in Iceland."

20. Paul, "Microsoft Japan Tested a Four-Day Work Week and Productivity Jumped by 40%," 5.

21. Muoio, "A New Report Slams Tesla Working Conditions, Claims Employees Have Suffered Twice as many serious injuries."

22. Lambert, "Elon Musk Says He Will Perform Same Tasks as Tesla Workers Getting Injured in the Factory."

23. American Association of University Women, "AAUW Analysis of U.S. Census Bureau and U.S. Bureau of Labor Statistics Gender Pay Gap Data Reveals Little Progress."

24. Kolhatkar, "The Tech Industry's Gender-Discrimination Problem."

25. Stahl, "Leading by Example to Close the gender pay gap."

26. Schwantes, "The CEO of Salesforce Found Out His Female Employees Were Paid Less Than Men. His Response Is a Priceless Leadership Lesson."

27. Ford, "5 Ways to Honor and Advance Equal Pay."

28. Ibid.

29. Dobbin, Frank, and Kalev, "Training Programs and Reporting Systems Won't End Sexual Harassment." Promoting More Women Will," 687–702.

30. Mckinsey & Co, Leanin.org, "Women in the Workplace 2023."
31. Ibid.
32. Ibid.
33. Hunt, Layton, and Prince, "Why Diversity Matters."
34. Richard et al., "Employing an Innovation Strategy in Racially Diverse Workforces," 107–126.
35. Ibid.

Chapter 7

1. Mclain and Pendell, "Why Trust in Leaders Is Faltering and How to Gain It Back."
2. Covey and Merrill, *The Speed of Trust.*
3. Goodell, "Steve Jobs in 1994."
4. Villarreal, "Assuming positive intent—the secret weapon to surviving the holiday season."
5. Helgesen, "Work and (Not vs.) Love."
6. Guest Blogger, "Bad Boss Index: 1,000 Employees Name Worst Manager Behaviors [Infographic]."
7. Folkman, "It's All About Me! What Happens When a Leader Takes All the Credit?."
8. Veneziale, "The Power List 2017."
9. Ibid.
10. Monroe, "Cheryl Bachelder—Servant Leadership As A Catalyst for Culture Change."
11. MacArthur, "The MacArthur New Testament Commentary."
12. Sheridan, *Chief Joy Officer.*
13. Bettencourt, "*Triumph of the Heart.*"
14. Bock, "*Work Rules!.*"
15. Clark, "Intel's Culture Needed Fixing."
16. Schwantes, "Personal communication."
17. Ibid.
18. Grant, *Brené Brown on What Vulnerability Isn't* [Video].

References

"Dozens Of Former "Ellen Show" Employees Say Executive Producers Engaged In Rampant Sexual Misconduct And Harassment." *BuzzFeed News*. Accessed June, 2023. www.buzzfeednews.com/article/krystieyandoli/ex-ellen-show-employees-sexual-misconduct-allegations.

"Ford Factory Workers Get 40-hour Week." *History.com*, November 13, 2009. www.history.com/this-day-in-history/ford-factory-workers-get-40-hour-week.

"Toxic Culture Is Driving the Great Resignation*," MIT Sloan Management Review*. Accessed June, 2023. https://sloanreview.mit.edu/article/toxic-culture-is-driving-the-great-resignation/.

"Whole Foods' John Mackey on Capitalism's Moral Code." *Harvard Business Review*. Accessed July 26, 2023.

American Association of University Women. 2023. "AAUW Analysis of U.S. Census Bureau and U.S. Bureau of Labor Statistics Gender Pay Gap Data Reveals Little Progress." September 2023. Accessed April 1, 2024. www.aauw.org/resources/news/media/press-releases/aauw-analysis-of-u-s-census-bureau-and-u-s-bureau-of-labor-statistics-gender-pay-gap-data-reveals-little-progress/.

Ancona, D., H. Bresman., and K. Kaeufer. 2002. "The Comparative Advantage of X-Teams." *MIT Sloan Management Review.*

Author. 2019. *Business Roundtable Redefines the Purpose of a Corporation to Promote 'An Economy That Serves All Americans.'* Washington, DC: Business Roundtable. www.businessroundtable.org/business-roundtable-redefines-the-purpose-of-a-corporation-to-promote-an-economy-that-serves-all-americans.

Barsade, S. 2014. "What's Love Got to Do With It?" *IEDP Developing Leaders*. October 2014. www.iedp.com/articles/what-s-love-got-to-do-with-it/.

Barsade, S.G. and O.A. O'Neill. 2014. "What's Love Got to Do With It? A Longitudinal Study of the Culture of Companionate Love and Employee and Client Outcomes in the Long-Term Care Setting." *Administrative Science Quarterly* 59: 551–598.

Beck, A.C. 2013. "Eufear: Embracing Our fears' Positivity." *Issuu*. August 11, 2013, https://issuu.com/andrewcolinbeck/docs/eufear.

Bettencourt, M. F. 2016. *Triumph of the Heart: Forgiveness in an Unforgiving World*. Penguin.

Bock, L. 2015. *Work Rules!: Insights from Inside Google that Will Transform How You live and lead*. Twelve.

Brainy Quote. *The World's Largest Quotation Site*. www.brainyquote.com/quotes/vince_lombardi_786499.

Brooks, A. W. and Gino, F. 2015. "Asking Advice Makes a Good Impression." *Scientific American Mind* 26(2): 26–27.

Brown, B. 2013. "The Power of Vulnerability". *https://youtu.be/sXSjc-pbXk4?si=6-3-ck8CngLwQ-l3*.

Bryant, A. 2017. "I've Interviewed Hundreds of CEOs. They All Share This One Habit of Mind." *LinkedIn*, November 2017. www.linkedin.com/pulse/ive-interviewed-hundreds-ceos-all-share-one-habit-mind-adam-bryant/.

Cava, M.D. 2017. "Microsoft's Satya Nadella is Counting on Culture Shock to Drive Growth." *USA Today*. www.usatoday.com/story/tech/news/2017/02/20/microsofts-satya-nadella-counting-culture-shock-drive-growth/98011388/.

Chancellor, J., S. Margolis., B.K. Jacobs and S. Lyubomirsky. 2018. "Everyday Prosociality in the Workplace: The Reinforcing Benefits of Giving, Getting, and Glimpsing." *Emotion* (4):507–517. doi: 10.1037/emo0000321. Epub 2017 Jun 5. PMID: 28581323.

Chapman, B. and R. Sisodia. 2015. *Everybody Matters: The Extraordinary Power of Caring for Your People Like Family*. New York, NY: Portfolio/Penguin. p. 9.

Chen, T.P. 2024. "Remote Workers Are Losing Out on Promotions, New Data Shows." *The Wall Street Journal*. January 2024. www.wsj.com/lifestyle/careers/remote-workers-are-losing-out-on-promotions-8219ec63.

Cigna. 2020. *Loneliness And The Workplace: 2020 U.S. Report*. www.cigna.com/static/www-cigna-com/docs/about-us/newsroom/studies-and-reports/combatting-loneliness/cigna-2020-loneliness-report.pdf.

Clark, D. 2020. "Intel's Culture Needed Fixing. Its C.E.O. Is Shaking Things Up." *The New York Times*. www.nytimes.com/2020/03/01/technology/intel-culture-robert-swan.html.

Coyle, D. 2022. *The Culture Playbook: 60 Highly Effective Actions to Help Your Group Succeed*. Bantam.

Crowley, M.C. "Why Engagement Happens In Employees' Hearts, Not Their Minds."

Crowley, M.C. 2015. "Why Engagement Happens In Employees' Hearts, Not Their Minds." *Fast Company*. www.fastcompany.com/3041948/why-engagement-happens-in-employeess-hearts-not-their-minds.

Covey, S. M. and R.R. Merrill. 2006. *The Speed of Trust: The One Thing That Changes Everything*. Simon and Schuster.

Cunningham, L. 2014. "Trying to Change the World Bank." *The Washington Post*, April 10, 2014. www.washingtonpost.com/news/on-leadership/wp/2014/04/10/trying-to-change-the-world-bank/.

De Vries, M.F.R.K. 2023. "Why It's So Hard to Ask for Help." *Harvard Business Review*, July-August 2023. https://hbr.org/2023/07/why-its-so-hard-to-ask-for-help.

Deffler, S. A., M.R. Leary and R.H. Hoyle. 2016. "Knowing What You Know: Intellectual Humility and Judgments of Recognition Memory." *Personality and Individual Differences* 96: 255–259.

Dobbin, F. and A. Kalev. 2017. "Training Programs and Reporting Systems Won't End Sexual Harassment. Promoting more women will." *Harvard Business Review* 70(4): 687–702.

Dunlop, A., M. Pankowski., G. Marriner., S. Hatfield., and K. Starodub. 2023. *Hey bosses: Here's what Gen Z actually wants at work.* Deloitte Digital.

Durose, M. R., A.D. Cooper., and H.N. Snyder. 2014. *Recidivism of Prisoners Released in 30 States in 2005: Patterns from 2005 to 2010.* Vol. 28. Washington, DC: US Department of Justice, Office of Justice Programs, Bureau of Justice Statistics.

Dutton, J. E., R. Quinn., and R. Pasick. 2002. *The Heart of Reuters.* Center for Positive Organizational Scholarship, University of Michigan.

Encyclopedia.com. 2018. "Norman Schwarzkopf." August 18, 2018. www.encyclopedia.com/people/history/us-history-biographies/h-norman-schwarzkopf.

Engelberg, M. 2023. "The Violence in Your Business Language Diminishes You and Your Company." *Inc.*, January 2023. www.inc.com/moshe-engelberg/the-violence-in-your-business-language-diminishes-you-your-company.html.

Fitzgerald, A. 2020. "Barbara Walters Interviews General Norman Schwarzkopf (20/20)." *YouTube*, September 26, 2020. www.youtube.com/watch?v=2C6c66Kkevw&t=17s.

Flynn, F. J and V.K.B. Lake. 2008. "If You Need Help, Just Ask: Underestimating Compliance With Direct Requests for Help." *Journal of Personality and Social Psychology* 95(1): 128–143. https://doi.org/10.1037/0022-3514.95.1.128.

Folkman, J. 2017. "It's All About Me! What Happens When A Leader Takes All The Credit?." *Forbes.* www.forbes.com/sites/joefolkman/2017/11/10/its-all-about-me-what-happens-when-a-leader-takes-all-the-credit/?sh=3c062f12312e.

Ford, M.Q. 2023. "5 Ways To Honor and Advance Equal Pay," *Salesforce 360 Blog.* www.salesforce.com/blog/equal-pay-day/.

Fourmy, R. 2023. "Why Executives Need to Practice Vulnerable Leadership—and How to Do It." *DDI.* www.ddiworld.com/blog/vulnerable-leadership.

Francesca, G. 2018. "The Business Case for Curiosity." *Harvard Business Review* 96(5): 48–57.

Francesca, G. 2018. "Why curiosity matters." *Harvard Business Review*: 47–61.

Fredrickson, B. 2013. *Love 2.0: Creating Happiness and Health in Moments of Connection.* New York, NY: PLUME/Penguin Group.

Friedman, M.1970. "A Friedman Doctrine—The Social Responsibility of Business Is to Increase Its Profits." *The New York Times*, September 13, 1970. www.nytimes.com/1970/09/13/archives/a-friedman-doctrine-the-social-responsibility-of-business-is-to.html.

Future of Work Reinvented: Designing a win-win workplace for employees and employers. Gartner. www.gartner.com/en/insights/future-of-work#.

Geller, D. and P.A. Bamberger. 2012. "The Impact of Help Seeking on Individual Task Performance: The Moderating Effect of Help Seekers' Logics of Action." *Journal of Applied Psychology* 97(2): 487–497. https://doi.org/10.1037/a0026014.

Gerut, A. Host. 2019. "CEO Corner with Garry Ridge, CEO of WD-40 Company." *Small-Cap Institute Presents* Podcast, February 2019. https://smallcapinstitute.com/ceo-corner-with-garry-ridge-ceo-of-wd-40-company/.

Gino, Francesca. "Why curiosity matters."

Grant, A. 2021. "Brené Brown on What Vulnerability Isn't." *Taken for Granted*. www.ted.com/talks/taken_for_granted_brene_brown_on_what_vulnerability_isn_t.Grant, H. 2018. "How to Get the Help You Need." *Harvard Business Review* 96: 142–145.

Goodell, J. 2011. "Steve Jobs in 1994: The Rolling Stone Interview." *Rolling Stone*. www.rollingstone.com/culture/culture-news/steve-jobs-in-1994-the-rolling-stone-interview-231132/ accessed 5/13/24.

Guest blogger. 2019. "Bad Boss Index: 1,000 Employees Name Worst Manager Behaviors." *BambooHR*. www.bamboohr.com/blog/bad-boss-index-the-worst-boss-behaviors-according-to-employees-infographic.

Haidt, J. 2003. "Elevation and the Positive Psychology of Morality." In *Flourishing: Positive Psychology and the Life Well-Lived* , edited by Keyes C.L.M. and J. Haidt: 275–289. American Psychological Association. https://doi.org/10.1037/10594-012.

Hansen, M. T. 2018. *Great at work: How top performers do less, work better, and achieve more*. Simon and Schuster.

Harter. J. 2022. "Percent Who Feel Employer Cares About Their Wellbeing Plummets." *Gallup Workplace*. www.gallup.com/workplace/390776/percent-feel-employer-cares-wellbeing-plummets.aspx.

Harvard University. 2021. *Loneliness in America: How the Pandemic has Deepened an Epidemic of Loneliness and What We Can Do About It*. Accessed May 13, 2021. https://mcc.gse.harvard.edu/reports/loneliness-in-america.

Helgesen, S. 2023. "Work and (not vs.) Love." *Substack*. https://allrise.substack.com/p/work-and-not-vs-love.

Hunt, D.V., L. Dennis., and P. Sara. 2015. "Why Diversity Matters." *McKinsey & Company*.

James W.S. and D.M. Frick. 2009. *Seven Pillars of Servant Leadership: Practicing the Wisdom of Leading by Serving*. Mahwah: Paulist Press.

Kashdan, T. B., C.N. DeWall., R.S. Pond., P.J. Silvia., N.M. Lambert., F.D. Fincham., and A.A. Savostyanova, et al. 2013. "Curiosity Protects Against Interpersonal Aggression: Cross-Sectional, Daily Process, and Behavioral Evidence. *Journal of personality* 81(1): 87–102. https://doi.org/10.1111/j.1467-6494.2012.00783.x.

Kashdan, T. B., P.E. McKnight., F.D. Fincham., and P. Rose. 2011. "When Curiosity Breeds Intimacy: Taking Advantage of Intimacy Opportunities and Transforming Boring conversations." *Journal of personality* 79(6): 1369–1402. https://doi.org/10.1111/j.1467-6494.2010.00697.x.

Lambert, F. 2017. "Elon Musk Says He Will Perform Same Tasks as Tesla Workers Getting Injured in the Factory." *Electrek*. https://electrek.co/2017/06/02/elon-musk-tesla-injury-factory/.

LEADx. "Richard Branson's 7 Secrets To Leadership." https://cdn.leadx.org/wp-content/uploads/2017/06/LEADx-Branson-Leadership-Secrets-v1b.pdf.

Lemoine, G.J., C.A. Hartnell, and H. Leroy. 2019. "Taking Stock of Moral Approaches to Leadership: An Integrative Review of Ethical, Authentic, and Servant Leadership." *ANNALS* 13: 148–187. https://doi.org/10.5465/annals.2016.0121.

Lewis, T., F. Amini., and R. Lannon. *A General Theory of Love*. New York, NY: Vintage Books/Random House.

Lucas, S. 2024. "Costco Employees Just Voted to Unionize. The Company's Response Is Remarkable." *Inc.*, January 4, 2024. www.inc.com/suzanne-lucas/costco-employees-vote-unionize-company-response-remarkable.html.

Luscombe, R. 2017. "At least 80 People Form Human Chain to Rescue Stranded Group in Gulf of Mexico." *The Guardian*. Accessed October 31, 2013. www.theguardian.com/us-news/2017/jul/11/80-people-form-human-chain-rescue-gulf-of-mexico-florida.

Lynch, S. 2015. "Why Your Workplace Might Be Killing You." *Stanford Graduate School of Business*, February 23, 2015. www.gsb.stanford.edu/insights/why-your-workplace-might-be-killing-you.

MacArthur, J. 1984. *The MacArthur New Testament Commentary*.

Marchwinski, C. 2015. "Rich Sheridan on How to Succeed by Building a Strong Learning Culture." *Lean Enterprise Institute*, January 27, 2015. www.lean.org/the-lean-post/articles/rich-sheridan-on-how-to-succeed-by-building-a-strong-learning-culture/.

Marr, J. C., S. Thau., K. Aquino, K and L.J. Barclay. 2012. "Do I Want to Know? How the Motivation to Acquire Relationship-Threatening Information in Groups Contributes to Paranoid Thought, Suspicion Behavior, and Social

Rejection." *Organizational Behavior and Human Decision Processes* 117(2): 285–297.

McGregor, J. 2018. "This Professor Says the Workplace Is the Fifth Leading Cause of Death in the U.S." *The Washington Post.* March 22, 2018. https://beta. washingtonpost.com/news/on-leadership/wp/2018/03/22/this-professor-says-the-workplace-is-the-fifth-leading-cause-of-death-in-the-u-s/.

Mckinsey & Co, Leanin.org. 2023. *Women in the Workplace 2023.* Accessed April 2, 2024. https://sgffmedia.s3.amazonaws.com/sgff_r1eHetbDYb/ Women+in+the+Workplace+2023_+Designed+Report.pdf.

Mclain. D. and R. Pendell. 2023. "Why Trust in Leaders Is Faltering and How to Gain It Back." *Gallup.* www.gallup.com/workplace/473738/why-trust-leaders-faltering-gain-back.aspx.

Monroe, K. host. 2015. "Cheryl Bachelder - Servant Leadership As A Catalyst for Culture Change." *Cairnway podcast.* www.mixcloud.com/cairnway-podcast/ cheryl-bachelder-servant-leadership-as-a-catalyst-for-culture-change/.

Muoio, D. 2017. "A New Report Slams Tesla Working Conditions, Claims Employees Have Suffered Twice As Many Serious Injuries." *Business Insider.* .www.businessinsider.com/tesla-injuries-rates-higher-industry-average-worksafe-2017-5.

Nyberg. A., L. Alfredsson, T. Theorell, et al. 2009. "Managerial Leadership and Ischaemic Heart Disease Among Employees: The Swedish WOLF Study." *Occupational and Environmental Medicine* 66: 51–5.

Ornish, D. 2010. "Creating a High Trust Organization." *HuffPost.* www.huffpost. com/entry/creating-the-high-trust-o_b_497589.

Ostroff, C., L.E. Atwater and B.J. Feinberg. 2004. "Understanding Self-Other Agreement: A Look at Rater and Ratee Characteristics, Context, and Outcomes." *Personnel Psychology* 57(2): 333–375. https://doi. org/10.1111/j.1744-6570.2004.tb02494.x.

Paul, K. 2019. "Microsoft Japan Tested A Four-Day Work Week and Productivity Jumped By 40%." *The Guardian,* 5.

Porter, T., C.R. Baldwin, M.T.Warren, E.D. Murray, K.C. Bronk, M.J.C Forgeard, N.E. Snow, et al. 2022. "Clarifying the Content of Intellectual Humility: A Systematic Review and Integrative Framework." *Journal of Personality Assessment* 104(5): 573–585. DOI: 10.1080/00223891.2021.1975725.

Richard, O., A. McMillan., K. Chadwick., and S. Dwyer. 2003. "Employing An Innovation Strategy in Racially Diverse Workforces: Effects On Firm Performance." *Group & Organization Management* 28(1): 107–126. https:// doi.org/10.1177/1059601102250022.

Sala, F. 2003. "Executive Blind Spots: Discrepancies Between Self-and Other-Ratings." *Consulting Psychology Journal: Practice and Research* 55(4): 222.

Schaubroeck, J. and L.S. Fink. 1998. "Facilitating and Inhibiting Effects of Job Control and Social Support on Stress Outcomes and Role Behavior: A Contingency Model." *Journal of Organizational Behavior: The International Journal of Industrial, Occupational and Organizational Psychology and Behavior* 19(2): 167–195. https://doi.org/10.1002/(SICI)1099-1379(199803)19:2<167::AID-JOB831>3.0.CO;2-T.

Schawbel, D. 2018. *Back to Human: How Great Leaders Create Connection in the Age of Isolation*. Boston: Da Capo Lifelong Books.

Schwantes, M. 2018. "The CEO of Salesforce Found Out His Female Employees Were Paid Less Than Men. His Response Is a Priceless Leadership Lesson." *Inc.*, July 2018, www.inc.com/marcel-schwantes/the-ceo-of-salesforce-found-out-female-employees-are-paid-less-than-men-his-response-is-a-priceless-leadership-lesson.html.

Schwantes, M. 2018. "This Best-Selling Leadership Expert Reveals the Simple Habits That Separate Successful People From Everyone Else." *Inc.,* May 2018. www.inc.com/marcel-schwantes/this-best-selling-leadership-expert-reveals-simple-habits-that-separate-successful-people-from-everyone-else.html.

Schwantes, M. 2019. "Personal Communication." February 28, 2019.

Schwantes, M. Host. 2019. "Are Women Better Leaders, with Tomas Chamorro-Premuzic." *Love in Action podcast,* June 1, 2019. www.marcelschwantes.com/tomas-chamorro-premuzic/.

Seppala, E. 2014. "What Bosses Gain by Being Vulnerable." *Harvard business review*. 2–5.

Sheelah, K. 2017. "The Tech Industry's Gender-Discrimination Problem." *The New Yorker*, 13.Sheridan, R. 2018. *Chief Joy Officer: How Great Leaders Elevate Human Energy and Eliminate Fear*. Penguin.

Shuit, D.P. 1993. "Delancey Street Rehab Center to Open in L.A." *Los Angeles Times*. Accessed March 27, 2024. www.latimes.com/archives/la-xpm-1993-05-20-me-37496-story.html.Sinar, E., R. Wellins., M. Paese., A. Smith., and B. Watt, B. 2016. "High-Resolution Leadership: A Synthesis of 15,000 Assessments into How Leaders Shape the Business Landscape." *Development Dimensions International, Inc.*

Stahl, L. 2018. "Leading By Example to Close the Gender Pay Gap." *CBS News*, April 2018, www.cbsnews.com/news/salesforce-ceo-marc-benioff-leading-by-example-to-close-the-gender-pay-gap/.

Sutton, A. 2016. "Measuring the Effects of Self-Awareness: Construction of the Self-Awareness Outcomes Questionnaire." *Europe's journal of psychology* 12(4): 645.

The Silicon Valley Historical Association. 2011. "Steve Jobs on Failure." *YouTube*, October 31, 2011. www.youtube.com/watch?v=zkTf0LmDqKI.

TheCoach. 2013. "Reverse Mentoring." *YouTube*, September 14, 2013. www.youtube.com/watch?v=Pux40FNW9lk.

Thorbecke, C. 2023. "Zoom Will Lay Off 1,300 Employees and CEO is Taking a Massive Pay Cut." *CNN Business*. www.cnn.com/2023/02/07/tech/zoom-layoffs/index.html.

US Department of Health and Human Services. 2023. "New Surgeon General Advisory Raises Alarm about the Devastating Impact of the Epidemic of Loneliness and Isolation in the United States."

Veneziale, M. 2017. "The Power List 2017: Cheryl Bachelder." *Nation's Restaurant News*. www.nrn.com/nrn-50/power-list-2017-cheryl-bachelder.

Vianello, M., E.M. Galliani., and J. Haidt. 2010. "Elevation At Work: The Effects of Leaders' Moral Excellence." *The Journal of Positive Psychology* 5(5): 390–411. http://dx.doi.org/10.1080/17439760.2010.516764.

Villarreal, C. 2018. "Assuming Positive Intent- The Secret Weapon to Surviving the Holiday Season." *Medium*. https://medium.com/@drvillarreal/assuming-positive-intent-the-secret-weapon-to-surviving-the-holiday-season-153ac68296b3.

Virginia, L. and R. Sigurdardottir. 2021. "The Shorter Work Week Really Worked in Iceland: Here's How." *Bloomberg*. www.bloomberg.com/news/articles/2021-10-14/the-shorter-work-week-really-worked-in-iceland-here-s-how.

Walsh, D. 2018. "The Workplace Is Killing People and Nobody Cares," *Stanford Graduate School of Business*. March 15, 2018. www.gsb.stanford.edu/insights/workplace-killing-people-nobody-cares.

Weiner, J. 2012. "Managing Compassionately." *LinkedIn Pulse*. Accessed November 16, 2023. www.linkedin.com/pulse/20121015034012-22330283-managing-compassionately/.

Weiner, Jeff @jeffweiner. 2017. "Big Misconception About Managing Compassionately is that it's a 'Soft' Skill. Most Compassionate People I Know Are Typically the Strongest." *Twitter*. October 7, 2017. https://twitter.com/jeffweiner/status/916303636380176384?ref_src=twsrc%5Etfw.

Weller. C. 2017. "Forget the 9 to 5—Research Suggests There's a Case for the 3-Hour Workday." *Business Insider*. www.businessinsider.com/8-hour-workday-may-be-5-hours-too-long-research-suggests-2017-9.

Wright, J. C., T. Nadelhoffer., T. Perini., A. Langville., M. Echols and K. Venezia. 2017. "The Psychological Significance of Humility." *The Journal of Positive Psychology* 12(1): 3–12.

Zaki, J. "How to Sustain Your Empathy in Difficult Times."

Zaki, J. 2019. *The war for kindness: Building empathy in a fractured world*. New York, NY: Crown.

Zaki, J. 2024. "How to Sustain Your Empathy in Difficult Times." *Harvard Business Review*. https://hbr.org/2024/01/how-to-sustain-your-empathy-in-difficult-times.

About the Author

Marcel Schwantes is a respected leadership expert and author who explores the power of actionable love as a crucial business leadership skill. As an executive coach and keynote speaker with widely read syndicated columns and a top-ranked podcast, he demonstrates how leading with love can improve employee retention, boost engagement, help with team building, and achieve outstanding performance in the workplace. Discover proven business strategies and compelling evidence on the transformative power of humane leadership by following Marcel Schwantes.

JOIN MARCEL ON SUBSTACK

Index

www.ingramcontent.com/pod-product-compliance
Lightning Source LLC
Chambersburg PA
CBHW061154220326
41599CB00025B/4478

9 781637 427828